SUCCESS,

YOUR DREAM AND YOU

A Guide To Personal Marketing

SUCCESS,
YOUR DREAM AND
YOU

A Guide To Personal Marketing

Patricia J. Raskin

ROUNDTABLE
—— Publishing, Inc. ——

Library of Congress Cataloging-in-Publication Data

Raskin, Patricia J.

Success, your dream, and you / Patricia J. Raskin.

p. cm.

Includes bibliographical references.

ISBN 0-915677-51-2

1. Success in business 2. Self-realization 3. Title

Hf5386.R163 1991

650. 1-dc20   90-52808 CIP

FIRST EDITION

10 9 8 7 6 5 4 3 2 1

ACKNOWLEDGMENTS

I want to acknowledge the following people who have made this book possible:

My parents, Elaine and Melvin Raskin, who made me very, very strong.

My daughter Laura Shmishkiss, who gave me the freedom and space to do this work.

My loving husband, Antonio M. Carbonell, M.D., who spent many hours into the night helping me with ideas and words.

My best friend, Ellen Garber Rosow, who has been my "soul sister" since we were seven years old, and whose wisdom and guidance has helped me understand the kalidescope of my life and put the pieces of the puzzle together.

My loving and patient friend, Kathleen Stem, who has been my model of ease, elegance, and grace.

My friend and mentor, Mel Goldberg, who, as an author and publisher, always encouraged and supported my work, and was a key contributor to the birth of this book.

My friend, Joan-Ellen Foyder, whose guiding light, encouragement, and valuable suggestions always lifted my spirits and my pen.

My friend, teacher, and model of wellness, John Travis, M.D.

My first collaborator, Barbara Terman, who translated my ideas into the chapter on intuition.

This book is dedicated to

my beautiful daughter Laura,

and my loving husband Antonio.

CONTENTS

CONTENTS

FOREWORD

How many times have you sat back and daydreamed about how wonderful life could be if you only had a job you loved, complete financial security and a generally healthy, happy experience?

Would you like someone to help turn those dreams into reality?

Patricia Raskin is waiting to hand you a set of keys that will unlock the special doorways of opportunity along your chosen pathway.

You need to take the steps . . . to act.

Patricia's guidance, methods, tools, suggestions and ideas were born from experience, which is the source of their profound value. So when you apply them to your own unique experience, you are getting much more than the same stale "creation advice" and "success programming tips" that currently flood the marketplace.

This is a complete, sensible guide to business success that is based on solid business techniques and concepts. Married with personal awareness and a firm desire to change, the results you achieve can be breathtaking.

She should know. Her success – and this book – were simple seed ideas a couple of years ago. I watched her nurture her dream, hit many roadblocks and yet form it into a present reality. Here is information you can trust, because she's done it all. And this is material you can easily incorporate into your own experience. I marvel at how she seems to speak to me on a one-on-one level. I know you will feel the same.

Of course, nothing happens without doing it. Take that first, and sometimes hardest, step. Patricia will guide you through a fascinating process that begins with some serious self-exploration to help create a core directed vision. You will then proceed to learn how to access networking and communications channels and build supporting, nurturing structures and situations. Hit a roadblock? No problem, it is just a self-created method of steering you accurately and help you refine your chosen pathway. Patricia will show you how to turn what seems like disappointment into a helpful learning experience.

Remember that the trip is truly more important than the ultimate destination. As Patricia says, "the process is never static, but is always fluid and changing." And, in the process, you will find your success.

It is always good to have a wise, knowing and experienced guide along for the ride. Patricia has handed you the keys. Now get started!

– Paul Zuromski, Publisher & Editor-in-Chief
Body, Mind, Spirit Magazine
Providence, Rhode Island
1991

INTRODUCTION

As we approach the next century, we are facing exciting possibilities. We are coming out of isolation. Networking is here to stay and entrepreneurs, business owners, and managers are actively seeking support from their colleagues. No longer are decisions made solely at the top of an organization. More and more mid-level management staff and line people are participating in decision making. Call it new dimensions in customer service or service vision, people are being brought together to support each other and increase profits as a result of sharing forces rather than opposing them. The new customer service orientation is really a deeper orientation toward cooperation. From that perspective, competition becomes a way to encourage stimulation and movement instead of annihilating the opponent.

Home-based businesses continue to multiply, and the focus on customer service becomes even stronger. Customers and clients do not only want personal attention and empathy from their service providers, they expect it. In the coming years, we will be working towards retaining our clients – not just finding new ways to acquire them. The emphasis is on quality control, focus groups, added value, and support systems.

As the corporate structure and nuclear family has become decentralized as our mobility has increased with technological advances, some of our essential human needs have gotten lost in the process. As John Naisbitt states in *Megatrends 2000*, "The most exciting breakthroughs of the 21st century will occur not because of technology but because of an expanding concept of what it means to be human." So many of us have been left to search for the basic needs of nurturing and intimacy that

achievement
external rewards

we often substitute achievement and external rewards as a way to fill the void. However, self-nurturing, self-love, and self-acceptance are essential parts of creating a vision that brings you internal happiness as well as external success. ✓ Having faith in vision comes from a deep belief and trust of whatever we conceive we can bring into reality.

environment

✓ Winning environments provide the support system needed to propel you toward your goals. One cannot work in a vacuum and create a winning environment. Finding the right networks is an essential part of creating the support system. However, as technology advances in telecommunications, not only will you have to use your intuition in shorter amounts of time, but, in addition, you will need to extract human tone and feelings from the equipment. In addition to the frustrations of cancelled appointments, you now have to deal with computer shutdowns, modem and FAX delays. So creating winning environments and support systems involves developing a new respect for the telecommunications systems because it has become a large part of the support system.

When you communicate, it is not only important to understand your clients and customers points of view, but to take your own point of view into consideration. If the

BOTH NEEDS ME!

✓ client's need for help and understanding is met by the provider with similar needs, a bonding can occur that goes beyond creating a win-win relationship. This fusion of both parties' intent can contribute toward a collective consciousness for new growth.

Although positive thinking plays an important role in this, it has become an over-used phrase. The answer to so many questions has been, "think positively." And yet – it is just that effort to be positive in our thoughts and purpose that enables us to create the desired results in our lives. What would happen if suddenly a new picture came across our television screens and newspapers . . . one that told the stories of the achievers, awards, triumphs, and joys, of the people working together toward a common goal? What kind of world would we have if we used our intuition and understanding of ourselves and others to join together and create powerful and positive results? The response to these questions may be tinged with cynicism and skepticism as many tout that reality is filled with problems, catastrophes and suffering. However, "the stuff that dreams are made of" is "the stuff" that you visualize and believe can happen. That comes from the inner pictures and descriptions you paint in your visions.

And you have the choice as to whether your pictures will be positive or negative. All the resources to reinforce either a positive or negative vision are available. The choice is up to you. John Naisbitt and Patricia Aburdene go on to say in *Megatrends 2000*, "Humanity will probably not be rescued deus ex machina (from without) . . . the answers will have to come from us (from within). . . . Apocalypse or Golden Age. The choice is ours. As we approach the beginning of the 3rd millennium, the way we address these questions will define what it means to be human."

In the context of finding the answers from within to create your own "golden age," I have created a 5 P formula for actualizing your success and dream. The words are Purpose, Planning, Passion, Persistence, and Patience.

Purpose - It is here that you define your dream and create your vision. Here is where you answer the questions, "What are my goals and what do I want to accomplish?" And "How is my purpose connected to my overall vision?" I believe that part of your purpose is loving what you do, and staying true to your values. This may mean releasing a client, but then, you have the ability to draw in a new client, and one more aligned with your values. When you deal with clients, customers and colleagues always check within yourself to see if your purpose is a reflection of what he or she needs. And you can create a winning environment where conflict and struggle is reduced by matching your needs to those of the client and fulfilling your own purpose by meeting the needs of the client.

Planning – Your purpose must be translated into a plan, one that is coherent not just to you, but to others as well. This means putting together a business plan that will define your market, state your goals and objectives (including financial goals), and outline your action plan.

It also means doing your research and pricing your service within the market range in your area. Remember not to omit the most important of the research – you. Count the number of hours you spend on each project when determining your fees. Your labor is a very important part of the equation.

Another part of planning is to maintain your professional image. This includes the way you deal with clients, the way you dress, the words you use, your record keeping and your office space. We often become so involved in what we are doing that we forget the mundane details. However, it is carrying out those details by yourself or with with staff support that helps to maintain your focus. An important component of maintaining focus is to assess your goals and create new ones at least once a year. And in this assessment, create your own forecast by answering the questions: "What direction do I want my business to take? Where do I want to be in six months and in one year? What are my new financial goals?"

The following points are covered in corporate planning. I have interpreted the terms to apply in an entrepreneurial setting:

General management: running the day-to-day operation, using your time management skills which includes creating new goals, targeting new clients, promotional campaigns, and financial forecasts.

Strategic planning: planning for your growth in six months on paper.

Organizational development: training your staff to align their vision to your vision and to use the necessary skills to implement your goals.

Research and development: reading periodicals in your field, understanding new market needs, new products and services in your field, and creating surveys to test your ideas.

Marketing: the process of creating the awareness of your product or service and meeting the customer needs through such vehicles as advertising, public relations, promotional campaigns and the media.

Sales: actually making the transaction happen between you and your client or customer.

Human resources: selecting the right personnel, dealing with personnel wages, benefits, and issues.

Finance and accounting: keeping track of receivables and payables, which may mean hiring a bookkeeper or accountant.

Operations: dealing with the tools such as manuals, computer programs, and electronic systems that make the business operate.

These technical terms can be translated on paper into your own language by stating their personal application to your business. You may not know exactly where your business will be in six months, but, by writing down your goals with the intent of bringing them into reality in the specified period of time, you create the business affirmation to make it happen.

Passion – There's a lot of truth behind the lyric, "do your passion and make it happen." For passion is the driving force behind putting your purpose and plan into action. And, when you are passionate, commitment and motivation are automatic. Passion comes in like a big wave and sweeps you to your destination. I'm not sure that passion can be developed. I feel that it comes from a voice deep within you that must come to the surface and be heard. And the voice gets louder and louder, often to the point of explosion – until it finds a way to be expressed. The positive side of passion is that you don't have to try. Its exciting energy creates a life of its own and it transforms work into pure joy.

Persistence – Passion is great. But what happens during the difficult times when you, who are the motivator, are not motivated and your spirits are not spirited? That's when you can bring your persistence in to help you along. An important part of this process is getting the support of friends, books, nature, as well as using your own inner resources to persist through hard times. Writing and saying affirmations will also help to create, transmit, and actualize those wishes and dreams. Affirming where you are and how far you've traveled gives you the acknowledgment and encouragement to go on. Mistakes indicate a choice of wrong timing, wrong strategy, or wrong market. Persistence means having the courage to look at your mistakes, then reassess and move forward in a new direction. To find new direction, you can reach out by joining organizations that support your vision and look for contacts who will help spread the word about your business. Breaking down those large tasks into manageable pieces will help you prevent procrastination and complete projects.

Patience – Last but not least – and sometimes the greatest word of all – is patience. It's not easy to wait for the right things to happen, but this waiting time can be a most creative learning time. For it is during these pauses that you create new ideas. You have the opportunity to restore your balance by shifting activities and reflecting upon your process. I feel that success depends on how well you can develop and maintain a balance among your many roles. Work, play, sleep, relationships, hobbies, and fun are all vital parts to a balanced life.

You can learn how to visualize the process by using the creative waiting time to pause and look at where you are. Patience doesn't mean stopping. It means allowing and watching the process unfold. It teaches you to stop, wait and listen to your intuition for guidance. And it pushes you gently to understand, evaluate and appreciate the situation. It also gives you time to replenish, renew yourself, refuel your passion, while anticipating the excitement of achieving the long term goal.

XVI

It is during those "patient pauses" each day that you ✓ *PATIENT PAUSES* can spend time reviewing your successes and lessons and plan how you can attract more of what you need. You can extend this valuable attribute of patience when dealing with clients by thinking like a child and asking yourself, "How can I explain my product or service, slowly, lovingly, and with simple words?" Our clients need to hear the simple explanations that we often overlook, while quickly explaining our products and services in great technical detail. Patience may be the one quality that forces us to slow down, assess our position, change strategy, and create a new plan.

It is possible to create an environment where your clients will walk away smiling because you have made a positive impact on their lives by giving a part of yourself. But first, you need to understand how your internal mechanism works.

Ruth Ross, in her book *Prospering Woman*, states nine laws of prosperity. I believe in them so much, use them in my own life, and feel they are so related to personal success that I am including them here.

LAWS OF PROSPERITY

1: Law of Self-Awareness: "When we know who we are and what we want, we can have what we want in life."

2: Law of Wanting: "Experiencing choice means knowing what we want and why we want it."

3: Law of Planning: "Without planning there is no consistent prosperity."

4: Law of Releasing: "We must get rid of what we don't want to make room for what we do want."

5: Law of Compensation: "There is a price for everything and we must always pay."

6: Law of Attraction: "We attract what we are."

7: Law of Visualization: "We become what we imagine, positive or negative."

8: Law of Affirmation: "We become what we want to be by believing and affirming that we already are."

✓ 9: Law of Loving: "Whatever we want for ourselves, we must also want for others."

7 success steps

I have created seven steps which I feel will bring success into your life.

Step 1. Making your dream happen is no more than seeing and believing every part of your dream daily.

Step 2. Winning business relationships happen when your purpose matches the needs of the client.

Step 3. Telling your own truth without blame and listening to others "is what opens the door to positive communication with your clients ."

Step 4. Some of the best business decisions come from using your intuition . . . listening to your own inner voice.

Step 5. It's important to find and use the marketing vehicles and tools that target your market and, at the same time, meet your own needs.

Step 6. You carry your value system wherever you go. In order to achieve personal fulfillment at work, it is necessary that your values are in alignment with those of your company and organization.

Step 7. Placing yourself in winning environments reinforces your vision and moves you closer to fulfilling your dream.

Success, Your Dream and You is my attempt to bring light, love, cooperation, and peace into the workplace. It really is a book about relationships and how one can create positive and healthy relationships within the workplace. The relationship has to start with you because you bring yourself to the workplace. Personal awareness and a desire to change become catalysts for personal transformation. And personal transformation affects everything you do wherever you are.

Part of creating health and balance is to take each of the suggestions in this book step-by-step. Try new things, use what works, and give yourself credit for each accomplishment. Your process is the most powerful piece, because it is you. Your process is never static, but it is always fluid and changing. Sometimes the process presents what seem to be overwhelming challenges. But remember, you

NEVER ISOLATED
HIGHER GUIDANCE

✓ are never isolated. Your higher guidance is always available to open up your intuitive channels.

It is my hope that you can bring your personal light
into the workplace to illuminate the lives of others. By
sharing your own process and inspiring others to create
their own success, you become a powerful catalyst for
transforming dreams into reality.

1

Your Inner Image

*M*ost people have an "image" that comes from the outside. A good deal of time and energy goes into maintaining this image. When you create an image you desire, you escape the frustration of trying to be someone else. As you mold and shape your image, you are continually involved in self-examination and self-perception. At times this may seem narcissistic and selfish. But paying close attention to your inner voice is absolutely vital to creating and believing in your image.

Once you have created something that is in harmony with your true thoughts and emotions, you can move on to the next step – ego detachment. Your feelings, talents, and dedication go into shaping your work of art. When you are finished, there should be a "new you," someone you can market, attach a price tag to, or even sell. You can also discern its strengths and weaknesses.

Ego detachment does not mean that you must separate your inner life and your work life. If you created your image with close attention to your inner thoughts and emotions, then you can detach the ego without worrying about losing touch. You can go on "automatic pilot," knowing that your actions are in sync with your attitudes and beliefs. If the situation changes, you'll know it. The symptoms might be physical, like tension headaches on the job, or just a general feeling that something isn't quite

re-attach ego

right. Then it is time to reattach the ego, re-examine the image, and decide what needs to be altered.

We all project different images. A baker "sees" the cake before it is baked and an architect envisions the house he builds. But sometimes we have more than one role in life, and more than one image. These images are like connecting threads that intertwine all the roles we play. This can sometimes be confusing.

For example, we may identify with an assertive role at work. Then, at home, we become gentle and compassionate with family or friends. Roles change on a daily basis.

DESIGNING THE PACKAGE

We must examine the different roles we play. It is a fascinating process to explore the inner world of images. I have seen the look of surprise on people as they begin to discover their qualities, as these images unravel. Recently, when I guested on a television talk show, the interviewer asked, "Tell me, Patricia, how do you package yourself?" At the time, it seemed like such a strange question, like "How do you find the right person in your life?" It was almost impossible for me to answer in a few short sentences. Then I thought about the question and realized the need to find a clear concise answer. That day I defined four images that most of us project in a typical day.

Image 1: Suiting Up

Here we prepare for the day. We put on our costume and assume a professional role before leaving the house. We look in a mirror to see that our clothes, hair and attire are intact. That's the easy part, because it's so obvious. However, we must go deeper to get the whole picture. Here's a way to do it. Close your eyes and "see" those special qualities you portray. You might see confidence, charisma, or efficiency. Or you might see compassion, competence, or sincerity. It is important not to see the negative parts of ourselves as we leave for the day, only the positive images. We must dwell on the outstanding and worthwhile aspects of our inner and outer selfs before we meet the business world.

Thoughts make things happen. The frame of mind in which we start our day directs the course of the day.

Image 2: The Octopus

The octopus represents the parts of us that constantly extend out to others. Look at the different tasks you perform during the work day. See yourself going through each task, and make a mental inventory of the day. Since days change, so do circumstances, and your inventory will change as well.

What makes your image so revealing is that it creates an instant view of your work and gives you an opportunity to extend or contract yourself, on a needs basis. As you rethink your qualities during the work day, you may find additional ones that you did not observe in the morning. That is all to the good as you will see.

Image 3: The Home Role

We return to our homes for refueling. I often use the image of a nest when describing the home role, but not everyone views their home in that way. You must create a picture of what your home means to you and describe the special qualities you display there. Perhaps you are a problem solver, an organizer, or a sensitive person willing to listen to the problems of others.

The strengths you display in the home may be quite different from your other images. You may surprise yourself when you actually think about your "home virtues." Most people don't give themselves enough credit for the strengths they use in family situations.

Image 4: Spreading Your Wings

The last image is your social role where social skills are used in activities with our friends and associates. This is the part of you that explores new horizons, makes new contacts, and brings you freedom and self-fulfillment.

As you read the list, think about the special qualities that show when you spread your social wings. These qualities are factors such as confidence, excellent communication skills, and energy. You probably have many qualities to choose from in this category.

CONNECTING LINKS

There is a connection between the images we portray. Find the constants that are present in your life roles. Then try to rise above the tendency to get stuck in a particular role, like home-maker or executive. You can rise above your separate images and identify qualities that are always part of you.

FINDING YOUR ESSENCE

Search for the qualities that were constant in all your images. If your lists differ, go back and search for qualities that are constant. These make up your essence. Now take the words that were the same in your lists and study them. You may find two or three words like caring and responsibility, intuition and compassion, or sincerity and creativity. This was a healing exercise for me because I was able to see my strengths on a daily basis: integrity, vision, faith, compassion. On my "down" days, I know my ideals and faith will stand by me.

We carry this essence with us. We travel with it along the waters of life, dropping anchor into our different images. For example, we drop anchor when we "suit up" in the morning or we may drop anchor when we express certain characteristics at work. We do the same at home. There are special qualities for each image, so remember to drop your anchor into each one. Then you are there and fully present in your image.

We are the constant. Our essence never changes. We must know and feel our essence in order to create our image. Our essence is our spiritual core and spiritual

backbone. It's our special contribution and celebration of life.

The key here is non-attachment. We become attached to the moment when we "drop our anchor." Then we move on in a non-attached state. This gives us the freedom to move. The following are examples of attachment, non-attachment, and freedom in each of the four images:

1. You attach to the quality of impeccability. You feel so in control and in charge. You now proceed to work and someone spills juice on your suit. The image is ruined. You begin to lose your confidence. Now bring in *essence*. What are your qualities beyond the ones in the mirror?

Let's say that your essence qualities are compassion, creativity, humor, and sincerity. You can use these qualities to make light of the situation and understand the other person's embarrassment.

2. Your most important quality at work is originality. Today you have to return twenty phone calls, write a structured plan for a client, and help your secretary categorize new information. None of this is original or creative and you feel a lack of energy and motivation. All of a sudden you attach these feelings to laziness and the rest of the day is spent in self-blame. Let's return to your essence, which is creativity, compassion, and humor. You can use your compassion to understand and accept your dislike of routine, or you can use your humor to laugh at yourself for being so serious about it. These essence qualities are really lifesavers.

3. It's easy to find those special qualities at home. If you're a parent or spouse, you are probably responsible, a problem solver, and an organizer. A person can fill many roles. And, if you're single, many of these same qualities still hold true.

How do people get stuck in roles? Here's an example. You are in the midst of preparing for a family gathering.

You have everything in order when suddenly you realize you have forgotten a promise to spend time with your best friend whom you usually meet at this time. How do you solve the dilemma? You bring in your essences and they go to work. Call the person and invite them into your activity so they can become part of it. Your sincerity and compassion will be obvious to your friend. Now everyone is happy and your party goes off as planned. There are many ways to use essence qualities. This is simply one example.

4. Our social images are often numerous. We could be playing sports, attending a movie or play, relaxing at a party, or walking on the beach with a friend. It is hard to find constant qualities for this role because the scene keeps changing. Let's look to a specific situation. My "spreading wings" take me to parties, sometimes in different cities. Often my social life is related to my work because this is where I meet my friends. In this role, my qualities are excellent listening, flexibility and confidence.

At one party, a guest antagonized me. I tried to use my skills, but eventually I made a sarcastic remark to the person. This certainly did not portray me as flexible and compassionate. I felt embarrassed, humiliated, and angry with myself for not being able to manage the situation. I began to introspect. What could I have done?

First, I had to learn to be more compassionate. My response was a natural reaction, but my integrity let me confront the issue with the person later on that evening. My vision gave me the insight to realize that I was human, and subject to human foibles. I learned greatly from that incident by looking inside to find the answer.

OUR EVER-FAITHFUL ESSENCE

Here are some rules to follow that may help you with your essence:

1. See the undesirable qualities emerging from your roles.

2. Stop, and call upon your essence qualities.
3. Use your essence for clarity and freedom from the claws of the image.
4. Do not become attached to one image.   Always keep the essence words in focus.

SELF-ESTEEM

The essential ingredient in your success pattern is self-esteem, a feeling of physical and mental well-being, self-worth, and self-concern.

Self-esteem can be perfected as a skill.   It is then in-corpo-rated into our being.   We must keep affirming our worth and eventually we will believe it.   Here are exercises to build self-esteem:

- Look in a mirror and see the beauty within you. Hold the image for five minutes.
- Ask a friend for support to bolster your self-es-teem.
- Review your daily achievements and special events in your life.
- List ten of your outstanding qualities.   Go back to the four images for suggestions.
- Write five positive phrases on cards and look at them often.

Building self-esteem is one of the most healing things we can do.   It takes such a short time and has such long term effects.   We also can internalize self-esteem, if we ask ourselves the following questions:

1. Do I deserve what I have? Do I deserve to have what I really want?
2. When I picture different images, do they feel comfortable?
3. Is the image I want close to me or far away?
4. When I want someone to care for me, is there a person who will assume that role?
5. Do I gravitate toward personal and professional situations that enrich my life?

If you answered "yes" to most of these questions, you are close to your visions. If you answered "no," the exercises in this book will show you ways to move toward your goals.

DEVELOPING CLEAR FOCUS

The more focussed we are, the more easily we can get what we want. Focussing means staying with one task and giving it your full attention. It means saturating yourself in the task at hand and immersing yourself in the moment. It means giving jobs your total being. It's like exercising a muscle until it feels exhausted.

Focussing sounds easy, but is often difficult to put into practice. The structure of our society is based on fluctuations, constant movement, and multifaceted approaches. We are often encouraged to do more than one thing at a time. However, there are ways to practice focus that will help to reinforce this natural state. One of the best ways is through meditation. For the beginner, an easy way is to choose one image and stay with it for as long as possible. When the mind brings in other images, simply say good-bye to them and bring back your original image.

The following are some exercises that will help you:
1. Stare at a glass. As your thoughts pour into the glass, see yourself emptying them. Keep emptying the glass until no more thoughts are left.
2. Hold your arms above your head while listening to music. Your senses will be heightened.
3. Count to fifty slowly as you exercise. Then count backwards to zero. Focus on the numbers and nothing else.

These exercises help put the mind into an altered state, clearing it of negative thoughts and emotions, and building a sense of inner strength and peace. Most importantly – stay with the glass, the music, and the numbers.

Bring your mind back into focus when it starts to wander. This is not easy, but, once you do it, it will help focus your mind while you are engaged in other activities.

CLEAR INNER IMAGES

Your image is what you see, feel and believe. You can change it by changing what you see, feel and believe. Everything we project outwardly is a manifestation of what's inside us. The more the inside is cultivated, the more we can build an outside image. It is difficult to package yourself when you don't have a clear understanding about what's in the package.

Remember what the interviewer asked me on television, "Patricia, how do you package yourself?" He meant that the external and internal images were one entity, and he wanted to know how I put them together. Let's take an example of the chiropractor. He seeks an image of strength and knowledge. If those qualities don't resonate to his patients, he will not present the proper package and the patient may lose confidence in his abilities.

As a lecturer, my external package must include poise, communication, knowledge and flexibility. I try to create those qualities within myself so I can project them externally to an audience. Once you know yourself, you can do the same thing, regardless of your profession or job responsibility.

2

Creating Your Vision

*O*ne of the major rules of transformational thinking is that we can do or create anything we desire. Nothing happens externally until we visualize and plan it internally. When we ignore internal planning, we give up the right to shape our destiny.

We must build our vision, step by step. Start at the finish line like a runner, and picture yourself winning before the race begins. We must have that visualization within ourselves because, as we take action, we have a starting point, an initial frame of reference.

I look at three parts of vision: The real: where you are in the here and now; the ideal, where you want to be; and, the steps needed to bridge the real and the ideal.

REAL VISIONS

Look at where you are in the here and now. The following steps can help create the real picture for yourself.

1. In your mind's eye, visualize yourself during the workday. Get a clear picture of how it looks.
2. Tune in to how it feels. Does it feel bumpy? Does it feel smooth? Does it feel peaceful? Does it feel chaotic? Does it feel organized?
3. What do you see? Do you see a person running in a scattered manner? Do you see organization and punctuality?

4. Do you hear the telephone ringing all the time or a lot of chatter?
5. Can you smell the secretary's perfume and taste the coffee in the office?

It is important to get a complete sense of where you are. This will help the vision become complete in your own mind.

THE IDEAL VISION

Next, let us look at the ideal scenario. If you could have exactly what you want, what would it look like? What is the ideal picture for you? Some of you may say, "Well, I don't know what the ideal is. I'm not really sure what I want." In *Positive Magic*, Marion Weinstein writes about the difference between essence and form. She says, "The qualities of life that you desire, such as health, happiness, love, or prosperity, are essences . . . The specific things that you want or need to make your life more comfortable . . . dishwasher, new suit, car, trip, are the forms." For example, the essence of your vision is that you are an innovator and a creative person. So being creative and innovative are essences. Using those qualities, you could start your own company or be a cartoonist – or even an actress. The cartoonist, actress, and entrepreneur are the forms of the vision.

So, if you don't know what you want to do, you can always tune into the qualities or essences of your vision. For example, one of my clients recently came to me and said, "I have done many different things. I've worked in the fields of public relations and I've worked as an accountant." He had drawn circles and diagrams of all kinds of things that he had done, but he wasn't clear about the essence of the vision. He knew that he wanted to be an innovator by improving the system and finding new and better ways to do things. The essence of his vision was to be an innovator. The new job would become the form of the vision. He could apply his organizational abilities, math skills, and his love for people to the specific job and, since he discovered the essence, the form would be easier to determine.

My vision is that I am a bridge between the mainstream world and transformational thinking. I bring those "new-age," or transformational thoughts, into the mainstream world as a writer, lecturer, consultant, and media host and producer. Those jobs are the forms of the vision. Although the form varies in function, in all areas I am applying principles of wellness, responsibility, and cooperation.

I have found essence and form extremely useful for my clients and myself. I would like to expand upon these concepts. The following are examples of essence and form:

> *Essence*: Freedom, Peace, Integrity, Prosperity, Pioneering, Elegance, Creativity, Discipline.
>
> *Form*: Salesperson, Country Store Owner, Physician, Inventor, Hotel Manager, Author, Teacher, Athlete.

When creating a vision, bring in the qualities of the four inner images discussed in Chapter 1. They are part of your inner image. If that image isn't clear, your external life will also not be clear. Job selection is dependent on paying attention to essence.

We choose qualities that fulfill us on a personal level. Choose the career that best fits your internal person. You will know when you find that job.

BRIDGING THE REAL AND THE IDEAL

We create visual images of real scenes. We get a picture in our mind of what life looks like now. Then we create in our heads the ideal picture, as if it were on a television screen. See the qualities or essences that are involved in actualizing your vision, such as delegating tasks to people. Then try to create a form around it, such as being a manager or store owner.

In bridging the real to the ideal, you are going to look

at the picture that is tangible. Now, visualize the ideal picture.   See these two pictures clearly in your mind and make a big space between them. Then, draw an imaginary bridge between the two pictures of the real and the ideal. See the words and the images in that bridge that will take you from where you are to where you want to be.

Let's look at some examples from people in my workshops. These words take you from "here" (where you are now) to the "ideal."

Examples of bridge words:

Determination	Courage
Self-education	Dedication
Decisiveness	Vibrancy
Clarity in vision	Perseverance

The interesting connection about these words is that most are what I call the internal or essence words. They are not form words, such as desk, bigger staff, or money. They come from our internal drive, which show that it is within us to get from the real to the ideal. Reaching our dream is not outside ourselves, not dependent on external factors. On the contrary, we make circumstances happen by using our internal resources.

Now, let's examine how you can apply your real situation in the workplace to create the ideal vision.

For example, Jeff, a marketing manager, has a staff of ten, a base of a $500,000 market, and United States-based clients. In the ideal, he sees himself promoted to Vice President of Marketing, his staff has tripled in size and his market base has increased to $2,000,000 on a worldwide level. In the bridge, the steps needed to get from the real to the ideal, Jeff feels that he needs to develop his vision.

UNBLOCKING VISIONS

Some of the words we need to get from the real to the ideal are: perseverance, determination, and decisiveness. Without these words, our visions can remain blocked. This often happens when certain patterns and old tapes from our childhood creep up and begin to destroy our internal visions. Three techniques for releasing personal blocks follow:

1. The Swish (Switch) Pattern

According to Richard Bandler in his book *Using Your Brain for a Change*, the Swish Pattern reprograms your mind by switching the pictures. Visualize the current non-desired picture in your mind, like an unfinished project. Now, have a tiny picture in your mind of what you want to switch to. Then swish (or switch) the two pictures, so that the tiny one becomes the big one, and conversely. The rest becomes easy.

Think of a difficult situation. See the negative and the positive outcomes. Then:

1. See the negative one on a large screen.
2. View the positive one on a small screen in the corner of your mind's eye.
3. See the negative vision grow smaller.
4. Enlarge the positive vision.

Now, the mind will accomplish the rest of the task.

2. Affirmations, Release, Trust

Affirmations are statements that affirm where you want to be. They are positive statements leading to our dreams, such as:

- "I am working in the right environment."
- "I am the right weight for my height."
- "I attract the right clients with integrity."
- "I make as many calls a day as I am able to comfortably accomplish."

The affirmations create the reality. Though we may not realize it, when we affirm something we want, we program our subconscious to lock the statements into our minds. If we say, for example, "I can't leave my job" or "I can't deal with my boss," we will receive in action exactly what we are thinking.

Book
"Superbeings"

One of my favorite books, which locks in positive affirmation, is *Superbeings*, by John Randolph Price. Price instructs the reader to visualize a vivid picture, using touch, smell, hearing and vision to create the reality. Then one makes the affirmation, and it is "stuck" in the subconscious mind.

3. Reality Checks

You can reinforce your vision by assessing your real situation and making a reality check on the positive events in your life. Cite your successes at work this week and write down these events. Next, write down what has not worked for you this week. Then compare the two lists. This exercise will allow you to see where you are and where you are not. Since many people exaggerate the negative, this exercise will give you the evidence you need to keep things in perspective.

A reality check worked for me when I was concerned that my work as a speaker and consultant was at an impasse. I listed the contacts I had made, the events in which I had participated, and the new opportunities that had been offered to me. Seeing that list showed me the reality of the situation and my anxiety and fears faded away.

Vision
DRAW
PICTURE
OVER
AGAIN
MANY
TIMES

Vision doesn't just happen from one set of affirmations and a few exercises. It is a process of reprogramming our brain and seeing, saying and drawing the picture over and over in our minds until it becomes part of who you are on a daily basis. As you live with the new pictures, you begin to live them and they become part of you.

GETTING RID OF THE OLD TAPES

There are times when you have said the affirmation, you have seen the positive picture and you are still hearing the old voices that block and negate your vision. The following affirmations from *Superbeings* are very effective in dealing with negative thoughts and fears.

"My true self wants me to have the fulfillment of my desires and nothing can stand in
the way of this infinite power."

"I have incredible confidence in myself to
keep the channel open for the manifestations of my desires."

Another exercise is to get comfortable, close your
eyes, take all the fears in your mind's eye and put them
into a big balloon, then watch them float away. If you
don't want to see the old tapes float, but want a more direct method of getting rid of them, visualize yourself taking the old tape in your hand and throwing it in the
garbage or incinerator. This will help you reduce the fears
and eventually eliminate them.

VISION, BLOCKS, AND CORRECTIONS
The two following business examples illustrate ways to
revitalize vision.

Example #1.
John is a sales manager who supervises people. His quo-
tas have dropped because his staff has very little guidance.
John's unmanageable schedule makes it nearly impossible
for him to train the group. He is aware he must meet with
the vice president of the company to discuss the problem,
but he puts the meeting off because he fears his boss may
not understand his needs. He assumes that asking for help
is a sign of weakness. Having created that picture in his
mind, the outcome of such a meeting would probably
meet John's expectations. Another way for him to
proceed would be to:
   1. See himself negotiating with the boss and devel-
      oping a staff plan (He has to switch his pictures).
   2. Visualizing the vocalization of a clear plan to his
      boss.
   3. Affirming that the meeting will go well.
Example #2.
Mary has been job hunting for months, averaging two

interviews per week. She presents herself well, but hasn't yet found the right position. She pictures obtaining that perfect job in her mind but is blocked by a fear of interviews. In order to release the fear vision, she does the following:

1. Affirms success and positive results at every interview.
2. Switches the tapes so that the fear tape becomes small and the success at the interview tape becomes large.
3. She writes down her affirmations of success.

OVERCOMPENSATION

When we have had a lot of negative programming, we may overcompensate by becoming obsessive about image, success, money or power. We may make it externally, but, internally, we are never satisfied. This may cause us to work harder, even compulsively, sometimes to the point of addiction. Even if we are successful, we have taken on the wrong image. Vision is created at the expense of happiness because, in our search for external success, we left behind the essential ingredient of internal success.

My personal vision of success is one which is free from compulsive behavior, bringing peace into one's life as well as prosperity. When you understand what makes you happy, you can create a vision that works for you. This is not a simple task. Many people spend their lives searching for a dream, only to find another rung on the ladder to be scaled.

I devote a lot of space in this book to the process of looking at your wants, your needs, your values. Those are the bricks to building the "business house of your dreams." With the bricks or building blocks in place, the house has a sturdy foundation and is not influenced by the "whims of the weather." In the same way, when your business values and desires are in place, you will have built a solid foundation that will weather changeable market conditions and differing opinions.

3

The QPN Model

Qualities stand for the features we display to our clients such as enthusiasm, knowledge, integrity, patience.
Purpose stands for our purpose in working with the client.
Needs stand for the needs of our client.

We create a "winning" situation when our *qualities* meet the *needs* of our client to fulfill a common *purpose*.

I n my marketing travels, I am often asked to help my clients find the right words to sell their service or product. Of course, if you are representing a product, you would have the description committed to memory. However, clients have different needs, and what serves one person might not serve another. Also, we often change our specific goals, depending upon the situation.

Although we believe in what we are selling, we often have to explain it on the spot without much time to think about to whom we are explaining it. When this happens, our product or service sounds generic and looses its personal touch. Have you even felt that the live words you were listening to sounded like a recorded message? What is most important to clients in dealing with service providers, health-care givers, and salespeople is that their needs be understood and met.

Whenever we present ourselves, we are selling ourselves. We have a choice as to what we wear, what we say, and how we explain our service or product. When we use our intuition to tune into the client and ourselves, we can create a picture of the situation. The picture alone will conjure up words that tell you what you see, hear, and feel from the client. The ingredients for your needs and those of the client are in those intuitive flashes, as well as in the data or facts that you have learned about the client and yourself.

The clearer we are about our own goals and needs, the easier it is to meet those of the client. Because once we know what we want, the client will either fit those general needs, or they won't. If they don't, we have the choice of staying with the client anyway or referring him or her to someone else. This understanding of our own positive qualities and goals, along with the understanding of the clients, is critical to the process of success.

I designed the QPN Model out of my own need to organize my thoughts clearly and quickly. I also needed a frame of reference to which to refer when I felt confused, frustrated, or stuck in my position. This chapter is devoted exclusively to the QPN Model, as I feel it is the basis for personal success in marketing. The QPN Model is applied in many chapters of this book. I use the Model in my workshops and seminars and participants apply it to their own professional situations. The QPN Model is easy to use and you will have the opportunity to apply it in the personal application at the end of this chapter.

YOUR QUALITIES

Your qualities are so much a part of you that you don't often stop to analyze them. And since you know all about your positive and negative qualities, why do they need to be explained? When people buy your product or utilize your service, they are buying you. The prospective client wants to know all those glowing qualities that might seem redundant or embarrassing for you to explain. And, they often want to know these qualities when they first meet with you. If the choice is between two practitioners with exactly the same skills, the one chosen will be the one who appeals to them in some way. That appeal could be looks, knowledge, empathy, an elegant visual space, or countless other qualities depending upon the client's needs.

I'd like to explain my concept of the word *qualities*. I compare qualities to features. For example, if you were to look for the features on a refrigerator before purchasing it, you might prefer extra cubic freezer space or an automatic ice maker. In the same way, what makes a person appealing to another in a professional situation are the qualities or features he or she displays.

In a situation where you are a service provider, your client needs to know what it is you have to offer. Here are a list of qualities clients admire:

1. Knowledge – you are highly skilled in your profession.
2. Trustworthiness – you do as you say.
3. Empathy – you care about your client's feelings.
4. Experience – you have been in your field for a substantial length of time.
5. Insight – you use intuition well.
6. Innovative – you pioneer new ideas.

There may be qualities we wish to hide from time to time, qualities that hold us back from our goals and dreams. Some of these are procrastination, fear, disorganization, and obsessive behavior. These are "weeds" in your garden. If they are not all picked, the whole garden can become overgrown with them. We are all susceptible to such negative qualities.

For example, we might become disorganized when we have inadequate space in which to store materials. This

Service provider	Provider's Purpose
Physician	• To heal the sick, and help bring a state of wellness into their lives.
Health practitioner	• To help people become more responsible for their own behavior.
Therapist	• To help people see their self worth,so that they realize their full potential.
Financial planner	• To help educate people about their finances while improving their position.
Lawyer	• To help people resolve their legal issues in a positive and balanced way.
Teacher	• To help students learn the skills they need to apply to their life work

Service provider	Client's Needs
Physician	• To understand symptoms, be treated and become well.
Health practitioner	• To learn more about behavior and take responsibility for his/her health.
Therapist	• To understand issues, deal with feelings, and integrate all these into his/her life.
Financial planner	• To create a plan that will help clients attain financial security.
Lawyer	• To have expert representation in legal issues and to resolve legal problems.
Teacher	• To learn the subject and the skills necessary to be successful in his or her work.

does not mean we are disorganized people under other circumstances. The same applies to procrastination. If we procrastinate with one issue, we may not do so in other avenues of our lives. All of us are susceptible to negative qualities given the wrong circumstances. We need to assess each situation separately, and not become attached to labels or qualities.

YOUR PURPOSE

Your purpose is your need to fully express yourself. You also must define your professional purpose. Purpose is not the job or the company you own. The job is the outcome of the purpose. It is important to understand your purpose because it is at the core of your work. Your goals and activities follow the purpose and set it into motion. All my activities in the past decade have set an example for my purpose.

Words sometimes push one's purpose into the future. Most people want their purpose to be now. Even if you don't accomplish all your goals, keep the vision constant. To achieve a sense of well-being, state the purpose as an affirmation. Then it becomes a bridge between transformation thinking and the mainstream business world. The purpose is always stated as an affirmation beginning "I AM" or "I HAVE."

THE CLIENT'S NEEDS

An integral part of the QPN Model is the N, or *Needs* component. Once we have established the qualities and purpose, it is then time to examine the needs of clients and customers. This is not always as obvious as it appears. There is often a hidden agenda behind the client's needs that becomes more apparent as one gains his trust. The N will answer the question, "What is the benefit to the client provided from my product or service?"

The client will have obvious needs, like needing the product the salesman sells, or needing the services of the accountant at tax time. However, the more we know about our client's inner needs, the better we are able to establish a rapport and to provide adequate services.

The first question in determining the needs of your clients is "Why do they need my services and how will they benefit from them?" You may answer with such phrases as: gaining financial security, achieving wellness, achieving and maintaining well-being, or succeeding in work. Here are other examples of how your assistance provides the right service to meet the needs of the client.

P = N, THE WINNING EQUATION

We all want to have our needs met. In the QPN Model, the winning part of the equation is when your purpose matches that of the client. Examples of purpose matching needs are:

1. The surgeon's *purpose* of mending the body and the patient's *need* to regain health.
2. The college professor's *purpose* to transmit information and to inspire students. The student's *need* to learn and integrate the information.
3. The salesman's *purpose* to sell the product and the consumer's *need* to use it.

These examples may seem like common sense, but the P=N equation is a good barometer of the climate of your business transactions. When P does not equal N, problems will arise that create a win/lose situation. For example, the surgeon needs to operate, but the patient is resistant. Or the college professor believes in his subject, but the student is taking the course only because it is required.

The foregoing situations can be transformed into winning events when one person changes his position and understands the needs of the service. In the case of the surgeon and patient, the patient begins to understand the need for surgery. Although fearing the process, he knows it is the best alternative. In the second case, the student may change his attitude while taking the course and experience the value in the teaching. What begins as a win/lose situation can end in winning for both parties. Being aware of your purpose, and the needs of the client, will help to determine your direction and the course of the relationship.

Q AND THE CLIENT

At the beginning of this chapter, I discussed the features of the refrigerator. In comparing this to meeting the needs of a client, you provide the client with many benefits. Qualities and needs are like features and benefits. A feature of the refrigerator is the ice-maker. It also has other features which make it palatable to the customer. In the same way, the service provider has many qualities and features. For example, let's say that your client needs fast and efficient service.

The benefit to the client is efficient delivery. Although one of your qualities is efficiency, if you show only empathy to the client, you are not providing him with the benefit he needs. It is important to select the right qualities to serve the client. I have developed a formula for this selection process called Q=N.

Going back to the example, let us say that you are efficient—Q. Does that meet the N—needs of the client? Yes, because in the this case efficiency is what the client requires. Empathy is the wrong quality. In using the Q=N Model, check to see if the qualities you use meet the client's needs by asking "Do these qualities match up to my client's needs?" If they don't, replace them with the qualities that do. Writing it down will help you to see the issues more clearly.

TARGETING YOUR MARKET

Let us now apply the Model to a specific market. Who are you trying to reach? Who do you want to buy your product or use your service? You might say, "Everybody," but we don't all have the same needs. Each market is different and it must be broken down into its component parts. If, for example, your product is a nutritional supplement, you must find specific groups or markets who need your product. These could be health clubs, athletes, corporate employees, or countless other groups. Each market has different needs and each one needs to be dealt with separately.

The most effective use of the QPN Model is to apply it to a specific market or client within that market. Your qualities will change depending upon the client's needs. Although your general purpose is usually consistent, the specifics change from market to market. The QPN Model varies from client to client and the Model may even change with the same client as his or her situation changes.

RESEARCHING THE MARKET

Once you have targeted the market, the next step is to understand what the market needs. In many cases, your market is your specific client. Knowing what that client needs requires research. I have defined two types of research: subjective and objective. *Objective research* deals with facts, data, and history. This information contains events that have occurred. Examples of objective research are corporate annual reports, a patient's medical history, school records, financial statements, and employment history. This information is necessary, but does not tell the whole story. *Subjective research* deals with intuition, feelings and events that have happened but are not recorded as data. It is based on your senses and the feelings you get from the situation. Examples of subjective research are messages you get from your intuition about the overall presence of the client or company during phone conversations, interviews, and meetings.

Information from subjective and objective research must be combined to give a complete picture of the client. Both subjective and objective components tell different parts of the story. It is up to you to decide how to use the information. To illustrate this point, let's look at your client, Corporation X. In determining the needs of your client, you read the annual reports and newsletters and find that the client is well established in the marketplace (objective research). On paper, the company looks ideal. However, after meeting with the decision makers, you realize that they are closed to new ideas and don't encourage creativity (subjective research). You now have to decide how important the internal aspects of the organization are to you. It is imperative to make decisions based on these facts, coupled with your intuition.

THE QPN MODEL IN ACTION

The following is an application of the QPN Model used by a consultant in a management consulting firm: The company is Edmund Box Company.

Objective Research: Annual report, written proposals, and monthly newsletter.

Subjective Research: Meetings with management at Edmund Box Company. Feedback from personal friends within the company.

Q – The consultant is focussed, persistent, knowledgeable.

P – The consultant's purpose is that he is creating a more efficient organizational structure for the Edmund Box Company.

N – Needs of the company are to increase sales by tightening the organizational structure.

Q=N – Client took four months to sign the contract with the consultant due to the latter's knowledge and his ability to stay focused and persistent in dealing with the client. These were the essential qualities in selling the client and maintaining the relationship.

P=N – The consultant's purpose is to create an efficient system for the client, which is exactly what the client needs.

USING THE QPN MODEL

The QPN Model can be used in any business situation. You need to write down what you think the client needs and to use your intuition in assessing the situation. If you feel the client will be resistant, try to visualize a harmonious situation prior to your first meeting. This harmonious thought will go a long way to keeping the situation a winning one for both parties.

If you feel resistance during the meeting, and find that your purpose is not in alignment with the client's needs, discuss it with them. If the client wants you to rush a job, there is a way to work out a winning situation using the QPN Model. Whatever the problem, there is a resolution for both you and the customer. You can learn to "tune in" and "stay in tune" with your clients, patients, and people with whom you deal on a daily basis.

We will explain how to apply the QPN Model in the following examples.

THE PARENT/TEACHER CONFERENCE

Mrs. Bell is a third grade teacher meeting with the mother of Johnny Jones, a bright, but underachieving student. The teacher is aware of the parents' concern, and she knows they want fast answers from her and better grades for Johnny. Mrs. Bell is patient in her approach and believes Johnny will succeed with understanding from both parties. The mother does not have patience, nor does she want to change her style or demands.

In the parent/teacher conference, the teacher used the QPN Model to deal with the situation. Gathering the facts was the Q, and giving the parent what she needed the N. Mrs. Bell's purpose (P) was to teach information, delivered according to each student's learning style. The teacher also knew that the child was bright and she felt he needed a more direct and aggressive approach from her. She wanted him to succeed.

In dealing with this situation, Mrs. Bell tried to show the parent the rationale behind her approach. For the parent to win, the teacher would have to demand better results from the student, which could cause him anxiety. For the teacher to win, the parents might have to lower their expectations. Up to this point, the teacher's purpose and the parents' needs were in conflict. In order to create a winning situation for both, the parents and teacher will have to share the same point of view, or make accommodations for differing points of view. The situation has a resolution. The teacher will introduce new activities that will help to expand the student's skills and the parents will do their part by meeting with the teacher on a periodic basis to discuss the child's progress. By using the QPN Model, the teacher was able to plan an effective strategy.

THE INSURANCE SALESMAN AND THE QPN MODEL

Bob represents a national insurance company. His major client is ZZ Corporation, for whom he writes health and fringe benefits for 3,000 employees. Bob deals with Mr. Daley, Vice President of Human Resources. Mr. Daley has decided to drop Bob's insurance company and move his business to another company, which surprises Bob.

The first thing Bob does is to assess the current financial picture of the corporation to determine how he can approach Mr. Daley. He believes the proposed change could be avoided, but has not kept track of Mr. Daley's changing needs because he has not communicated with his client on a regular basis. He asks for a meeting to discuss the issue. He knows the vice president's needs and so, after this first meeting, he matches those needs by proposing a way that Mr. Daley can remain covered by Bob's company.

Bob was not able to ulitile the proper qualities (Q) in the first meeting because he had not stayed current with this client's needs and, therefore, didn't meet the needs (N) of the new situation. But Bob was able to save his client because he presents his new program to Mr. Daley just in time after the first meeting. Bob learns an important lesson from this experience and develops a written system (P) for analyzing client needs (N) on a regular basis.

QPN
MODEL
✓

The QPN Model can be the key to your success and is the basis of this book. Remember that *Qualities* (Q) are your features such as enthusiasm, patience, efficiency, while *Purpose* (P) is your purpose in doing the work and expresses your needs. *Needs* (N) are the needs of your clients and customers. The needs tell your clients how your service will benefit them. The ideal situation is when your purpose matches the needs of the specific client, i.e. P=N, and when you find your specific qualities (Q) that match the needs (N) of your client. Remember that subjective research deals with intuition and feelings, while objective research is based on facts, data and history.

It is my hope that you can apply the QPN Model to your own work situations.

4

Applying The Model To The Vision

*T*rue self-marketing is a growth process, weaving together our skills with our attitudes. The QPN Model can help this process as it applies to the workplace. The following stories illustrate the way in which this can be done.

WINNING THE TOUGH DEAL

My close friend just negotiated a property settlement under very difficult circumstances. His chances for winning depended on calm strength. Before he met with the target group, he told me the positive outcomes that would occur. I wrote down his words. Everything happened just as he believed they would. He saw the people intuitively and set the tone for the meeting. This ability to look ahead took considerable belief on his part. He knew that only good would come from his opponents. When he believed that right action would take place for his highest good, he was able to create a winning environment that worked.

THE AIRPLANE STORY

Due to an airline's overbooking, I was recently offered complimentary airline tickets in exchange for taking a later flight. We had arrived at the airport earlier than anticipated and told the attendant that we would give up our seats if they were needed. As we boarded the plane, we heard that our tickets were not needed. But other people were giving up their seats and receiving the dividend. I spoke up. "Look, this isn't fair. We were the first to offer our seats." The airline personnel apologized, but did nothing. Then, at the last moment, the flight attendant approached us and said our seats were needed after all. The incident was the airline's mistake, but it worked to my benefit.

I'm usually not that assertive. I often sit back and think that things happen as they are supposed to happen. But I had visualized those free tickets and wanted them. Even though speaking up didn't work initially, the forces worked in my favor and I got the tickets anyway.

The desire and the drive to make something happen is based on the very strong belief and vision that it is already so.

The people who face rejection and who believe at face value those who tell them that their proposals aren't going to work, or their books aren't going to work, or their job isn't going to happen, will find their dream falling by the wayside. In order for the vision to manifest, it has to be locked into your internal system and become part of you. When this happens, doing your work in the world becomes a natural process.

Many times, the affirmations we say, such as "I am beautiful," "I am thin," or "I am doing well" don't hold. This is because it takes more than visualization and repetition of words to manifest our visions. You have to continue to live with the vision, to know in your heart and mind that your dreams will come true. This is a very important concept. What makes visualization and affirmations work is the intensity of the desire to satisfy our internal need and make the dream happen.

The experts tell us that a habit will become yours if practiced for at least thirty consecutive days. However, it's difficult to unlock the emotional state that contributes to unwanted habits. When you saturate your physical and emotional systems with the desired behaviors, and winning environments, it is easier to have faith in your affirmations and visualizations.

MAKING THE QPN MODEL WORK
Once you lock the vision into place and are ready to take action, you can implement the QPN Model over the phone, or in meetings with clients. List all your qualities because they may run the gamut from shy to outgoing. Then understand your internal purpose (P). Third, you need to know the N or needs of your potential clients. Now you can set up a situation and fill in the Q, the N, and the P, so that you create a winning situation for both parties.

RESEARCHING THE CLIENT'S NEEDS
Finding out the needs of your client requires subjective and objective research, discussed in Chapter 3. Subjective research is based on intuition – what does the client need? Objective research is based on history and data, like annual reports or medical files.

Examples:
1. Dick has prepared for his job interview. In doing the objective research, he has read Company M's annual report and newsletter and discovered that the sales are higher than any of their competitors, and that they are about to open in new markets.

Since Dick has not yet been into the company and doesn't know anyone there, the subjective research will become part of his interview. In the interview, the manager asks Dick questions that put him in a defensive position. He senses that people are not sharing, and are working in isolation in their offices. These feelings are subjective, but become major factors in making his job decision about Company M.

2. Jean also interviews for Company M. She has done the objective research by reading the established facts about the company. She has an advantage in doing the subjective research because her close friend in the company has told her that creativity is not encouraged.

In both examples, Dick and Jean take all of these objective and subjective factors into account. And, by doing the research, they get a complete picture of the job. Although the reputation and facts about the company are impressive to Jean, she knows that she needs a job in which her creative talents will be encouraged. She may still take the job if offered to her, knowing that she will have to compromise on creativity, but she was aware of this possibility at the outset and had time to explore other avenues for her creative expression. Having taken both the objective and subjective research into consideration, both Dick and Jean have a clearer picture of the company's status and can make stronger decisions.

APPLYING THE QPN MODEL AT WORK

Regardless of your job, you can apply the QPN Model to determine the needs of your client and the market. The process of applying the Model is explained in the following situations:

Examples:

1. Joan applied to a company for a job. She knew they were a fast growing organization and that her word processing skills were in demand. Joan prepared for the interview because she did her homework and knew what the company needed. After the interview, she surmised the following intuitive data:

- The atmosphere in the office was calm
- The secretary was friendly.
- People were working diligently.

- She learned the company's needs through the interview.

As she listened to the needs (N), described by the company official, Joan is able to respond by stating her achievements and accomplishments that apply to the new position. From the discussion, Joan is able to determine how her purpose (P) and goals match the company's needs (N) and if this job suits her.

If the job does not appeal to Joan, but the company makes her an offer, she can take the job, knowing that it is a stepping stone to a more desirable position. As long as she keeps this in mind, she will be aware that this is not a compromise, but a necessary and positive step to her future.

The more information you have about a company, the better your choices will be. The following is a list of questions to ask during the interview as part of the research:

- What skills are most important in this job?
- Where does the company see itself in the next two years?
- What type of personality is the company looking for?
- In what kind of environment will I, as the employee, be working?
- What are the growth opportunities?

These questions are an important part of your research and they are the ones that most often have to wait until you are face to face with the interviewer. Part of the research is writing these questions down and memorizing them, so that they appear to be spontaneous in the interview.

2. Ken is a sales representative on the road selling product for Company B. He reports to John, the sales manager. Ken meets his own purpose (P), and the needs (N) of his boss by keeping daily records of phone calls and appointments, kind of sales he made and feedback he re-

ceives. Ken's qualities (Q) that meet the needs of the company are his attention to detail, follow-up, product knowledge and enthusiasm.

So what do these qualities do for the company? If his attention to detail or enthusiasm were not valued by his boss and the company, they would not be of value in this situation. We have so many personal qualities from which to choose. It's matching the qualities to the needs that is important here.

Ken's purpose and the purpose of the company are aligned because both want to sell the product to increase the comfort of their customers. Here purpose (P) = needs (N) and Ken creates a winning situation between himself and the company. But Ken also has to meet the needs of his customers as well as his company. In this sense he becomes the middle man. His purpose is to sell the product so that he is fulfilling his purpose (P) and the client is getting what he needs (N). Therefore, P=N and a winning situation is produced. The more Ken develops rapport with the client and understands the client's changing needs, the greater the chances of opening the door for future transactions. Also, in developing rapport, Ken begins to understand which of his qualities work with that client (Q). For example, this client may require a lot of listening and problem solving approaches (Q=N). The QPN Model makes it easy to assess the situation and make it work for Ken and his clients.

3. In this scenario, the lawyer is representing the client in a domestic transaction. In meeting the needs of the client (N), the attorney has to understand that his own value system (P) comes into play. Different lawyers might have differing statements on the subject, all based on their individual value system. What will make or break the deal is the lawyer's sensitivity to the situation, and his ability to be objective about the possible outcomes.

That is why it is so important to find alignment between the lawyer's purpose (P) and the needs of the client

(N). If the attorney doesn't believe in the case (taking it for monetary reasons only), the lawyer and client both lose, because the lawyer cannot effectively defend a case in which he does not believe.

Intelligence, intuition, and integrity are the formula for keeping client relationships balanced.

EXTERNAL APPLICATIONS

External appearance is part of the QPN Model because the client's visual needs are important. Here are tips to create a better image:

1. Go to a color consultant to learn what your best colors are.
2. Utilize the services of beauticians and cosmeticians.
3. Find out about the dress code at work. It may be unspoken, but you have to know and understand the needs of the situation. It is possible to maintain your individuality while staying within the needs of the company, client, or situation.

Clothing reveals much about yourself. You cannot meet another person's needs at the expense of your own. If you work in an office where the employees wear cut-off jeans and you never wear jeans, you can dress casually and not sellout your personal dress code. Your clothing makes a statement about you and your purpose. Dress within your comfort level.

FOCUSSED SURRENDER

The last step in applying the vision is focussed surrender. You must let go and give up pushing, flowing with the energy that moves you toward your goals. Let your vision flow, otherwise the energy will remain stuck. As you work on your vision in the here and now, you are free to "let go" knowing that your images will take hold.

5

Using Your Intuition

*H*ow many times have you made a right decision based on a "gut feeling?" Intuition often shows itself in actual physical sensation – you can "see" the outcome, "feel" that something is right, or "hear a voice" telling you to trust your instincts.

Intuition is a hot topic in business today. Business schools and popular consultants are teaching courses using tuition in business decisions. In today's fast-paced environment, people who can make right decisions quickly and easily save time and energy.

WHAT IS INTUITION?

People often mistrust intuition because it seems to come from nowhere. "Give me the facts," they say, "not a lot of mumbo-jumbo about feelings." The truth is, although intuition may manifest itself in feelings and sensations, it doesn't come from nowhere. From birth, we accept and store information in our brains, much as a computer accepts input. When we make rational, logical decisions, we retrieve information, analyze it like a computer, and come to a decision.

Intuition separates human thinking from rational, logical, computer-like reasoning. Although it is based firmly on facts we have stored in our minds, intuition skips

39

the conscious, rational steps and appears immediately as the "gut feeling" – the actual physical sensation in the abdominal area – that tells you whether or not you are making the right decision.

Because it is based on facts, intuition is rarely wrong. Where many people fail with intuition is in refusing to listen to it. We become so accustomed to "thinking rationally" that we ignore and suppress the physical and emotional signs of intuition.

INTUITION AND STRESS

Intuition and stress are opposites. When we are under stress, we may become more "rational," pushing intuition into the background. Stress can cause physical problems, because we are suppressing our "gut" feelings. We can do detective work on our bodies to find out when stress has become more than we can bear. Stress symptoms do not come out of the air. They are triggered by thoughts and feelings. These symptoms are trying to tell you something about the pressures you are experiencing.

It is important to understand and monitor stress levels in order to become aware of imbalances. When under stress, we should try to use more intuition, rather than less. That doesn't mean ignoring important facts. It means taking into account all the facts.

The voice inside us tells us when we are not listening. Our behavior gives us the answers. When we don't listen to our intuition, we lose time, energy and efficiency.

LEARNING INTUITION

Everyone is born with the ability to be intuitive, but often it is bred out of us as we mature. Many people think it is more "adult" to make decisions based solely on external facts, leaving out emotion.

Ignoring intuition means ignoring one of the most important sources of factual information available to us.

Intuition is a *skill* that we can practice. Because all

the information we store in our brains is interrelated and based on our own experience, there is a synergy that occurs in the intuitive retrieval process. It is an automatic reflex that is triggered to relay the right information instantly, without conscious thinking. The more we use the process, the quicker it will occur. The more we practice it, the more adept we will become at recognizing what is true intuition, and what its signals are.

MIND MAPPING

Mind mapping was developed by Tony Buzan in England and has been used by many groups and corporations. The book, *Drawing On The Right Side Of The Brain*, by Betty Edwards, develops the "whole brain" approach and ties in with the concept of mind-mapping. A mind map is a pictorial representation of how the brain organizes information. It creates categories and is a way of putting ideas down on paper. Then intuition can "run wild." Mind-mapping can be used in any phase of business.

DEVELOPING INTUITION

There is no single, surefire way for everyone to develop intuition. Read the methods below, and choose the ones that work for you:

- Keep track of your "feelings" that something is going to happen. Write them down. See how many come true.
- Spend time with intuitive people. Watch how they do it.
- Find a quiet spot for uninterrupted thinking.
- Still the mind by meditating daily for at least fifteen minutes.
- Use repetitive exercise—running, cycling, swimming—to induce a trance–like state.

Benefits

Consider intuition another source of information – a source you can't always explain to others, but a source that does not lie.   When intuition contradicts "facts," you are faced with a tough decision. Take quite a lot of time to really listen to your intuition, and make sure that you are hearing it correctly. The benefits of using intuition include:

- building self-esteem and confidence in your own decisions;
- developing trust in self;
- helping you make decisions more quickly and decisively;
- strengthening your perceptiveness;
- opening your "data bank" of knowledge, allowing you to use all the facts; and
- keeping you from acting out of desperation or panic.

SHOULD HAVE KNOWN

Even those of us who speak and write about intuition are subject to occasional "panic" decisions and I'm no exception. It happened during a dry spell that all consultants suffer, when the phone isn't ringing, and you're convinced that the rest of the world has forgotten you're there. Out of desperation – a sure sign that I was suppressing my feelings – I hired a consultant to help me with my personal marketing. As always happens when I ignore my intuition, there was a red flag that I ignored, the warning that later made me say, "I should have known." And this red flag was a "biggie." The first words out of the consultant's mouth were, "Do you have $5,000?" Instead of asking what the money was for, I answered meekly, "I think I can get it." (I later found out he wanted me to buy a computer and start a newsletter.) By the time I started listening to my gut feelings, it was too late; I had already paid him a consulting fee. There was nothing to do but make the best of the situation, which I did. I got him to give me three sessions rather than the one he had offered, and I got some useful information from him. I also learned that the next time I should trust myself, that "dry spells" are only temporary. If I had trusted the "seeds" I had planted earlier, I could have enjoyed the brief time off from speaking engagements.

TIMING: INTUITION VS. PANIC

Developing superior intuitive skills means that you can often shortcircuit the decision-making process and know almost immediately what the best course of action will be. There's a fine line, however, between quick, intuitive decisions and panic. Often, when we're under pressure to decide, we can be swayed by factors that wouldn't influence us if we were thinking and feeling more clearly. How many times have you been fast-talked into buying something you later regretted?

There are many situations when a quick answer is important. And there are many times when we know instantly, without hesitation, what the right answer is. If you feel rushed and pressured, pay attention to your intuition. Don't decide until it *feels* right or until the logical evidence overrides your intuition.

ASSESSING INTUITION

Take a few minutes to think about the use of intuition. When was the last time you asked yourself, "How do I feel about this decision?" Do you routinely ignore your feelings because they don't always support the facts?

Often, when our sensations counteract logic, we try to talk ourselves out of having the feelings. If we're having a hard time working on a project, we may tell ourselves we're lazy and lack discipline.

Yet no one is inherently lazy and underachieving. We all want to do our best, and even the "laziest" among us will put forth incredible effort when we're doing something we love. How often have you worked so hard that you completely lost track of time? Wasn't it a time when you were working on something that excited you? These feelings mean something, and we ignore them at our peril.

CLUES

There are always clues that signal our need to change before we make a mistake. The following examples show some behavioral manifestations that indicate your intuition is trying to tell you something.

- You have trouble listening to others.
- You're smoking or drinking more, or your eating habits have changed for the worse.
- You consistently run late for several days in a row.
- You're having trouble starting or completing tasks.
- You get angry more easily than usual.

RISKS

Trusting your intuition can be scary at first, especially if you've gotten used to ignoring it for years. The risks involved in following your intuition include:

- fear that you're acting irrationally.
- requires stretching beyond your comfort zone.
- requires practice.
- requires developing a new type of self discipline.
- may call for change, often radical change.

There are times, of course, when we have to do what we "should" do, not what our intuition tells us we want to do. The important thing is to learn to recognize the difference. Constantly burying your own "right" feelings, in favor of obeying the "shoulds," indicates that something is seriously wrong. Either you need to reassess your own values, or you may need to reassess the situation. Why is it that your intuition is so out of sync with the things you do? What can you do to change your situation so that you can once again feel *right*?

Example:

- I should volunteer for a tutoring program.

- I feel that tutoring isn't really my strength.
- I will volunteer for another program that feels right for me.
- I should try the position offered to me.
- I feel that it's not really what I want.
- I will keep looking for what I really want.

RUN YOUR OWN MARATHONS

This story is from Barbara Terman, a professional writer from Chicago, Illinois, who collaborated with me in writing this chapter.

"For a jogger like me, running a marathon always looms as the ultimate challenge. No matter how faithfully I hit the trails, no matter how many 10K races I ran, I just didn't feel like a 'real runner' because I never ran a marathon.

"So I set my sights on the Marine Corps Marathon. After all, if you're going to run twenty-six miles, what better incentive than to have the course lined with tough looking Marines who won't let you drop out?

"Throughout the summer, I trained faithfully, running increasingly long runs every Sunday: twelve miles, fourteen miles, sixteen miles, eighteen miles. I found that the marathon training was taking my whole weekend. I had to go to bed early on Saturday, so that I could get up at 5:30 on Sunday morning and get in several hours of running before it got too hot. All day Sunday was spent recuperating.

"Finally, I worked up to twenty miles. For two weeks in a row I got up at the crack of dawn on Sunday to spend nearly four hours pounding the pavement. I fought blisters and boredom and just plain common sense, but I did finish the runs. My running friends encouraged me, always asking how the program was going.

"After the second twenty-miler, when I almost passed out in my plate at brunch, I began to seriously question what I was doing. After all, what was I trying to prove? Running twenty miles all by myself was actually a greater challenge than running twenty-six miles in the excitement of a major marathon, with thousands of fellow runners and spectators to encourage me, aid stations to provide water, and my husband waiting at the end. What I had accomplished that morning was enough. I knew I could do it, and I didn't really have to prove it to anyone else. I didn't want to devote every weekend for the next two months to re-proving something I already knew. So I decided to stop the program and not run the marathon after all.

"It wasn't easy to trust my intuition in this matter. My running friends couldn't understand at all. I seriously considered lying by telling them that an injury had forced me to quit.

"But I didn't. I tried to explain to them that I didn't *need* to run the Marine Corps Marathon – that my own Sunday morning marathons were enough. I felt like a real runner. I don't think they understood, but I didn't really expect them to. I knew it was the right decision anyway."

BALANCING LEFT AND RIGHT BRAIN

When learning to use intuition, a key word is balance. The left side of the brain is logical and linear. The right side is creative and intuitive. Our society has long stressed logical brain power over creativity. Eastern philosophies have encouraged the development of the right side of the brain. It is important to strike a balance between both hemispheres of the brain in our business and personal dealings.

PRACTICAL STRATEGIES USING INTUITION

Once you sharpen your intuition, you'll wonder how you ever got along without it. Read through the following experiences from meetings. As you walk into a group, do the following:

1. Mentally record your first impressions or sensations.
2. Notice the body language of the participants – alertness, slumping, fidgeting.

3. Are people on time?
4. Are people making eye contact with others?
5. Is the person who called the meeting clearly in command?
6. When group members speak, do their nonverbal clues match what they are saying?
7. Where does the power come from?

Use your intuition to find the answers to the preceding questions.

Interviews
When you visit a prospective employer or client, pay attention to the signals you receive.
The reception area. Do you feel welcome?
The person you are visiting. What is your first impression?
Eye Contact. Do people meet your gaze?
Do you feel free to express yourself?
Do people speak from the left or right side of the brain?

A Potential Partner
1. Is this person tense or relaxed? Is he comfortable in the new situation?
2. Is his voice relaxed?
3. Can you visualize him as a vital link in your organization?
4. Does he share your sense of purpose?

Sales
1. Is the buyer excited or, at least, interested?
2. Where is the enthusiasm coming from?
3. How about his tone of voice? Is it interested or bored?
4. What is the person's emotional state?

Relationships With Clients
1. Do you have rapport with clients?
2. How do clients see you?

3. How do they feel in your presence?
4. How is the atmosphere in your office?
5. How does the client react to your work?

Relationships With Staff
1. Do people hear what you say?
2. Do they see your points?
3. How do you feel in the presence of your staff?
4. Do people seem comfortable with you?
5. Do they ask questions willingly?

BUSINESS HUNCHES

Intuition can lead us to people who can help us in many ways. Try to evaluate flashes of intuition. If you "see" something happening in your "mind's eye," listen to it. These flashes are important; they mean something. Call the person visualized. Ask him or her to lunch. Over lunch, discuss the problem. Even if that person has nothing to do with the problems that are directly confronting you, he or she may be able to offer some valuable insight, or help you find the answer yourself.

Intuition can also help when you're dealing with people over the telephone. Sometimes you may be reluctant to call someone. For instance, I constantly send out mailings to prospective clients, which I follow up with phone calls. This is all very methodical, and I try to do it on a schedule, giving them time to receive the material, but not letting too much time go by before I call.

Sometimes, though, calling just doesn't *feel* right. I make up excuses not to pick up the phone, then berate myself for being "lazy" or "scared." The truth is, if, on a certain day, I don't feel like calling prospects, it probably won't work for me that day. My intuition can tell me when I'm most likely to be effective over the phone.

PURSUING INTUITION

Intuition as a business tool is very popular these days. Currently, there are many books that discuss how the internal, spontaneous retrieval of data from our computer minds is an essential part of our decision-making process.

If you are interested in exploring the topic of intuition further, there are several sources listed in the Appendix. Whether or not you choose to read more about intuition, I urge you to learn it, practice it, and use it. Intuitive thinking can help you break through old patterns of thinking to create a new wave of consciousness and blend new ideals into the existing framework of your life.

6

Winning Environments

*P*lacing yourself in winning environments is a simple concept, but may take some effort to apply in your situation. If you want to attract health, success, wealth, peace, comfort, and wisdom, find places where those qualities thrive. As the old saying goes, birds of a feather flock together. Stay with the birds that are compatible with you.

ATTRACTING WINNING QUALITIES

Since the idea of winning environments is so vital to positive growth, I would like to give examples of how to attract the qualities you desire.

Health
1. Spas are a good place to begin, if you are trying to develop sound, disciplined exercise habits.
2. Eat at restaurants that have a good selection of nutritious food.
3. Rediscover the natural energy found in parks, lakes, recreational areas, and other natural environments.
4. Select clothing made from natural fibers.
5. Join a group of people with positive attitudes.

Success

1. Everyone defines success differently. Decide what success means to you.
2. Read about the life of a successful person.
3. Success is a combination of happiness, financial security, accomplishment, and recognition. Which of these qualities have you achieved?
4. Get to know a person you admire professionally and emulate this person.

Wealth

1. Nothing is more inspirational than listening to financially successful people. Obtain some motivational tapes. Hear the story of Colonel Sanders, who went to hundreds of stores with his ideas before anyone listened to him.
2. There are many good books and magazines on money management. Try to read some of them. (See Appendix)
3. Find out what wealth is not. Many people are motivated by "get rich quick" schemes. You need to avoid them.
4 Find people who have combined wealth with peacefulness and joy. It is not an easy combination to find, but one that is worth searching for.

Peace

1. Peace is a sought after state of mind. Define what peace is to you.
2. Go back to nature. Resonate with the sounds and sights around you.
3. Go to an area where you feel joyous, such as the beach or the desert.
4. Find a place of spirituality and rejuvenate your soul.
5. Look for people who are peaceful in your job situation.

Comfort
1. Spend time with comforting people.
2. Find things that comfort you when the going gets rough.
3. Choose clothes that make you feel comfortable.
4. Find comforting people at work who will give you the strength to complete the task at hand with renewed motivation.

Knowledge
1. Go to experts in your field, through books, classes, or sharing with friends.
2. Knowledge comes from both positive and negative experiences. Understanding your mistakes and learning from them gives you knowledge.
3. Knowledge is everywhere. Model what you like and put away the rest.

Wisdom
1. Listen to the words of the sages. Take them in. Write down your favorite sayings.
2. Follow the advise of wise friends and counselors. Copy their examples.
3. Wisdom is timeless knowledge. Everything you learn, or have learned in the past, is potential wisdom.

You can create winning environments after you have internalized what you want. You must believe in your dream and visualize what you want it to be.

So, for example, let's say that you want to work in a creative environment with intuitive managers and people who value the process as well as the final product, but you are not clear about your role. You can begin to choose the necessary elements for the winning environment, such as being with people who work together as a team, where new ideas and innovative thinking are encouraged and where the overall vision is always at the forefront of the process. If that picture is in your winning environment, the right form will appear. I have found that my pictures are so powerful because the universe fills in the details with the right people and events.

And even if it feels like you are in the wrong environment, look again. There is always an essential element present to move you on to your next level of growth.

SMALL DOSES GO A LONG WAY

You may find yourself in a winning environment for a brief time. That experience is like an extra battery to recharge you when you get exhausted or discouraged. Small doses of good experience go a long way, so find people and situations that will infuse you with winning pictures of yourself.

ROLE MODELS

Copying a role model can be beneficial. But, be careful to copy only the role, if it pleases you, and not the person. It is sometimes valuable to select excellent characteristics of several role models to give you guidance in your own business career.

ATTRACTING WINNING ENVIRONMENTS

There are many places that send out harmonious feelings, like retreat centers throughout the country, where you can go to restore strength, energy, and vitality. Such winning centers are worth finding because we can't create them in our lives unless we experience them. You can create serenity anywhere – in your own home or even in your car.

The home is an extension of ourselves. The decor tells people how we feel about ourselves. The workplace also reflects the energy of the people. Many offices are simply little cubicles and have no feeling of integration or joy. You can create your own winning environment at work by being creative. Your workplace, like your home, reflects your energy. Whenever possible, bring pictures, posters, and small ornaments to the office. Pay attention to color and style in selecting office furniture. Do everything possible to keep your work environment pleasant and keyed to your personal tastes.

We use our five senses to pick up important information. Our sensory awareness is responsible for much of the intuitive information we receive. You can compose your winning environment in the workplace by tuning into your senses.

A TEN STEP WINNING PROCESS

Let's look at the practical side of things. When you are in a negative, non-winning environment, you can still visualize and create the environment you want. Your vision will not happen right away. But it will happen if you are patient.

Look at the following example:

Pamela worked for an advertising agency that produced nutritional and cosmetic products. She had worked with these products for years and was happy with her work environment. Her job consisted of writing ad copy for the products.

However, as she became involved in the operation of the agency, she discovered the company was promoting products for just the financial return. Half of her time was spent writing ad copy for other food products and she was constantly under deadlines. Although she was accepted for her belief in nutritional products, she was not encouraged by her boss and co-workers.

Let's follow the ten step process in this situation.
1. Pamela wanted creative freedom and a support system.
2. The one essential ingredient was that sales were all that counted with the company.
3. Pamela saw the staff coming together to discuss the nutritional products.
4. Pamela saw the situation as it was, with people

rushing to meet deadlines.

5. The two visions were diametrically opposed. The pieces needed to bring the two visions together involved movement, creativity, and sharing.

6. Pamela felt the pieces were not realistic. She could not visualize anyone in the agency moving in a direction that supported her vision. She saw the staff as rigid and stuck on one track.

7. She needed freedom, creativity and sharing. It was difficult for Pamela to see herself working in this sterile environment.

8. Pamela saw long term benefits of keeping an affiliation with the company.

9. Once she saw her long term goals clearly, she began looking for a way to create a winning situation for both herself and the agency.

10. She sought the alternative of becoming a consultant to the ad agency and keeping "their" client which would benefit the agency as well as Pamela. She also began searching for other clients in her field of expertise that would supplement her income.

Now, let's apply this process to your own situation:

1. Identify your most important ingredient in the winning work place.

2. Identify the one essential ingredient that is contributing to the environment the way it is now.

3. Visualize it the way you would like it to be.

4. Now, visualize the situation as it is.

5. Determine how far apart the two visions are. Is there a large gap between the two or are they closer together? Now fill in the gaps with the pieces that bring the two scenes together.

6. Next, ask yourself, "How realistic are these pieces? Can the changes occur so that my vision of the winning environment and the present one can become compatible?"

7. If the answer is yes, determine how.

8. If the answer is no, ask yourself how important those pictures are to you. Can you make an adjustment in your behavior and attitude so that you can live with the picture as it is?
9. Review your long term goals. Does the present situation support those goals, and, if so, is it worth keeping the affiliation with the company?
10. If the answer is yes, look for a strategy that will create a winning environment for you and the company. If the answer is no, begin to seek out alternatives. Make your move when you feel ready, from a position of clear thinking and strength – not out of frustration, despair, and anger.

SUPPORT IS EVERYTHING

Having supportive people in your environment makes the difference between success and failure. Support is often confused with pampering and indulgence. My definition of support is empowering a person to move to the next step of his or her path. Constructive criticism is a form of support when the recipient feels strengthened, revitalized and has found a new direction. However, it can quickly turn into destructive criticism when the ego is damaged in any way. When you suddenly don't feel good about who you are as a person after your friend or colleague has given you wise counsel, take a hard look at the source of the comments. Ego damage weakens self-esteem. And self-esteem is our emotional backbone.

About ten years ago, I attended a lecture where Sidney Simon, a well-known educator and author, was presenting his ideas. He gave a graphic example that I will never forget. He stressed that when you cross a street and see a car coming, you get out of the way. He asked, "Then why is it that when someone attacks you verbally, you lie down on the floor, open your arms and ask for more?"

Winners who get ahead by attacking other people's self-esteem are not winners. True winners help others win because they know that there is enough abundance for all of us.

> **Winning environments attract winning people. And winning people create more winning environments.**

CONVERTING IMPOSSIBLE ENVIRONMENTS

We sometimes find ourselves in surroundings we do not choose, such as bank lines or crowded buses. In these cases, it is better to avoid such situations by getting other people to do our errands, or to "tune out" the environment we don't like. A friend told me he learned to control his breathing in order to relax in New York's subway system. It also helped him to visualize clean, good energy surrounding him. We do have the ability to alter the energy around us through our thoughts.

The following exercises can help create winning environments:
1. See the situation as it is.
2. Decide that you can overcome it.
3. Visualize positive, clean, fresh energy.
4. Project this energy into your immediate area.
5. Breathe deeply and know that you are now in the protected environment.
6. If and when you begin to feel negatively, repeat the exercise.

The purpose in this chapter has been to create an awareness of the untapped positive elements of our environment, and to offer some practical tools to use in discovering those elements. Once we begin to understand the information we receive from our senses and intuition, we can use it to create balance and harmony in our work situations.

7

Money –
A True Success Tool

*W*e all know the benefits of money. The obvious reward is status, possessions, power, and success. There are the internal or intrinsic benefits of money that often go unnoticed and unclaimed. These are peace of mind, true enjoyment of external beauty and pleasures, the feeling of safety and security, and a true sense of achievement. There is a difference between success and achievement. Success is predetermined by the outside world and achievement is determined and felt by you.

The saying that money doesn't buy happiness is certainly true. But poverty doesn't either. Possessions alone breed emptiness and insatiability. The emptier we feel the more we want to fill ourselves with the things money can buy. The key to blending money and happiness is balance. And the key to balance is aligning our values with our visions.

When vision and values are synchronized, motivation, passion, and achievement are effortless. Money automatically follows. You may say that you love your work with a passion, but you have been struggling for years and can't seem to make a living. I say, "Look again." There is something blocking the path. Check your timing, your strategy, and the place you have chosen to work. One of these three things has a glitch somewhere. If you are not "making it happen" fast enough, check your internal time clock. The universe is a wonderful provider of what you need and it could mean that you need to restructure, have patience, or do something else to gain more skills for your higher purpose.

As we discussed in Chapter 2, both essence and form create our vision. The essence is the higher value of the work. It's our higher guidance giving us direction. The form always follows when we have established essence. If you want to make a lot of money doing what you love, then repeat your essence aloud and create a new form to match the essence that will bring you tangible money results. For example, my essence is the bridge between transformational and new age thinking and the mainstream world. The form of my work has changed many times from a personnel consultant to writer to television host to author. But the essence of my work has always remained constant and my message is constantly brought into the mainstream world.

It seems that so many of us who are conscious, love our work, and know our higher purposes are motivated. Then why is it that so many of us struggle with money? Often the struggle is with self-worth. We are worthy of internal richness, yet on some level we're not worthy of external richness. We live in a physical body; why can't we enjoy physical pleasures? Money brings peace of mind. All the jobs that looked so right on the surface did not work out. Instead, the ones that offered me what I really needed were offered to me.   I got what I needed by knowing the essence (qualities) of what I wanted, listening to my inner-guidance and being patient.

We are taught to view assets in the form of capital such as cash, credit, and property. However, there are hidden assets that create the power and positive force that money can provide. The true test of an asset is that it always gives you what you need. So, for example, the support of your friends, the furniture that was given to you, the office space you rented, and the extra time you were given to complete a project are all assets. These are the building blocks of creating money, just like vitamins and minerals are the building blocks of a healthy body. The money just doesn't appear, nor does the healthy body just appear. We carefully shape, mold and build step by step and grow inch by inch. We often forget the steps because we're so busy looking at the finished product.

THE MAGICAL MANIFESTATION OF THE COM-PUTER

One day I decided I needed a computer and didn't have the required capital. My family offered to buy me a word processor, but I declined. I just "felt" I would get what I needed. About a month later, a friend called me out of the blue and said that he had several computers. He offered one to me. I believe my thoughts actually produced that machine.

A PROSPEROUS GOOD-WILL PLACEMENT

A friend owns and operates a medical clinic. I took her to a party where she happened to meet the doctor she needed for the practice. Neither of us were looking consciously to make a placement, but out of her integrity she offered me medical services and airline tickets as compensation. I did not expect this "manifested" surprise.

The true test of an asset is always having what you need and then looking at the source that is meeting those needs.   So, for example, your friends, your education, your knowledge are all assets.

In addition to looking at our assets, we need to examine our internal definition of what money represents to us. For some, money is self-worth. For others, it is power. And for many, it is freedom. The problem is that, when the money is not in view, our freedom, power, and self-worth suddenly disappear into the green pieces of paper and don't reappear until we begin to generate cash again. When that much emphasis is placed on money, you can't enjoy the non-monetary attributes of power, freedom, and self-worth. Examples of freedom are being your own boss or walking on the beach. You create power by standing up for your own beliefs. An example of self-worth is taking the risk to create your own business. As you begin to see the things that you want to create, they will be yours.

I believe that the amount of money you create is highly dependent upon what you believe you deserve. When I hear people say, "I can't imagine having a car or a dress that costs so much money," I know that they have screened out conditions that their mind could not imagine. It's like saying, "I don't have a penny left." That affirmation will manifest itself if left in the consciousness to germinate. It would be better to think, "I am easily creating money to support my family." When this happens, the new idea will come to pass in due time.

YOU CAN MANIFEST WHAT YOU CAN IMAGINE

After we use the power of affirmations and visualization to manifest what we want in our mind's eye, there are some concrete tools that we can immediately put into practice. I learned the powerful concept of leverage from Marshall Thurber, a noted entrepreneur.

Leverage

Leverage, the basis for the success of millionaires, is the ability to produce maximum results, and reach the maximum amount of people, with minimal effort. Examples of using leverage in business would be writing a book that reaches thousands, presenting one lecture to hundreds of people, having a television or radio program, developing a franchise, and sending a newsletter to an established national mailing list.

Our assets can also be used to create leverage. For

example, contacts, courses, new information, innovative ideas that create a new and needed niche in the market-place, and networks, are all forms of leverage because they provide the components we need to create the system.

The following are examples of people who creatively choose and use leverage:

- A lawyer who specializes in an untapped area with tremendous market need (e.g. bankruptcy law).
- An entrepreneur who opens a franchise business in uncharted territory.
- A physician who owns or directs a clinic with various specialties.
- A lecturer who develops an audio cassette program that can be played anytime and anywhere.
- A businessman whose efforts are favorably written about in a major magazine.

Creating the above situations involves finding the right opportunities.

The following is a list of ways to tap into and find ways to leverage yourself in business:

- Doing demographic research – finding out where there is a need.
- Asking people who use your product or service for feedback.
- Visiting other operations and determining where you can fill the gaps.
- Networking with colleagues about current concerns and issues.
- Forming a think tank and developing ideas that fill a need.
- Meeting people who have created leverage successfully and copying them.

Remember that these ideas are the stepping stones to

prosperity. We can't discuss where and how to use money, until we find a way to create it.

PENNY WISE AND POUND FOOLISH

We can make a difference by the way we spend money. At times we save a few dollars and spare our own comfort. At other times, we spend lavishly. The key question is, "Will spending this money really make a difference to me or to another person?"

Corporate Image Story

John worked for a large corporation which boasted of professionalism and pride. On his first day of work, the manager wanted to take him to lunch, but the budget didn't permit it. Supplies were also curtailed for lack of funds. It was of concern to him that the company lacked professionalism when it came to employees, but gave that respect to clients. This action was both penny wise and pound foolish.

I believe this story is important because it says something about values and priorities. Unfortunately, money can be an emotional issue. In this case, the staff was not treated as valuable parts of the company. The irony is that it would have taken such a small amount of money to create such a large amount of good will.

The Pound Foolish Food Scenario

The corporate officers of Company XYZ visited one of their major divisions in New York and had an elaborate party in honor of the office opening. The purpose of the party was for senior executives and partners to meet and welcome the management and staff in the New York office.

Although the surroundings were beautiful, the party was formal and stilted. The staff of the New York office left feeling as unfamiliar with the executives from the corporate office as they did before the party.

The point of this story is that the staff didn't get what

they really wanted and needed: appreciation and support. The amount of food purchased could have been used better on a small intimate gathering with wine, cheese, and informal discussions.

When we spend our pennies, let us count the ways. The little purchases tell us about our big priorities and values. The truth is in the details.

SHARPENING MONEY SKILLS

If we look at money as a tool, we can take the emotional quality out of our perception. We are always at a disadvantage when we react to anything in a panic mode. By taking a self-supporting stance, we have time to think. So then let's think about ways to look at money as a tool. Any tool needs to be sharpened. We will explore tools that are subtle, yet easy to use, and provide invaluable resources.

MODEL THE MASTERS

If you are serious about making money, the best way to get information is straight from the horse's mouth. Go out to dinner with a successful entrepreneur and *listen*. This may take some time, since successful business people are usually overbooked. However, if you persist, befriend the secretary, and find a way to get in the door, the information forthcoming will be both sobering and inspiring. You'll surely know if this is the path for you.

SOLID RISKS VS. RISKY DEALS

Another skill to sharpen is the skill of taking risks. One of the things I learned about successful entrepreneurs is that they are risk takers. There is a big difference between risk and risky. Risk involves calculation, planning, and foresight. Risky adds the components of excitement and danger. Calculated risks are a part of life. Excitement and danger change the risk to risky and they present themselves only by our own willingness to let them in.

Now, sometimes there is a fine line between the two. You may want to gamble on the new house you are buying knowing that your income will increase within the next year. You and your accountant or financial planner can determine the risk involved, to a point. But there is a large element of faith and total belief in self and in your ability to generate the amount of money desired. The following are examples of taking financial risks and being financially risky:

Taking Financial Risks
- Investing in property in a good location, that has been endorsed by at least three people in the fields of real estate and financial planning.
- Investing a calculated amount of time to launch a new business.
- "Unexpectedly" buying a piece of land or property that is an unusual buy because of foreclosure, for example.

Risky Deals
- New research deals that look good – but have little substance, such as get rich schemes.
- Accepting a deal with only one opinion – especially the one of the seller.
- Borrowing money on a credit card with no foreseeable resources in the next year.
- Buying based solely on emotion and not fact.

KNOWING HOW AND WHEN TO USE ASSETS
Another money tool is the ability to use the assets around us. The greatest assets we have available to us are the people with the skills to create the money needed and make it grow. I'm referring to financial planners, accountants, tax attorneys, bankers, and investors. These people are great assets because they have the molds designed for the capital. They also have the ability to detach from the emotional side of money and look at the facts. I must add

that an essential ingredient is selecting the right person who understands your values and short and long term money goals.

We all have our own assets that can be utilized to trade for the services we need. For example, I have often exchanged a business consultation for printing services. We all have things that we can exchange. Determine the person's needs, and then try to match your skill to their need. If there is not a match, wait for the product you desire or pay for it.

I firmly believe that an exchange is only profitable if both parties have their needs met equally, creating a winning situation. My workshops have attracted astrologers who have often wanted to trade a chart reading for my consultation. The exchange worked well the first and second times. When the next astrologer approached me, I had to decline because I no longer needed this service. How many times have you traded things that you really didn't want or need? Accepting the right exchange is part of respecting yourself.

THE BUSINESS PLAN

Business plans are very important tools. They help you to focus, see your goals, set objectives, and look at the financial progression of your ideas. This is a good test of the validity of the project. Even if the plan ends up in the file, the exercise of writing the plan has all of the components of creating your dream by bringing it into reality on paper. Many of us have never written a business plan and often stop at that point. There are so many resources available that if you're really serious about your idea, the business plan will not only give you a clear picture of your project, but will also give you a sense of your commitment to the ideas.

There are times when a business plan is not needed. When working for someone else, a proposal of goals and job description are appropriate tools to show the employer that your position is compatible with his or her business.

TWO CRITICAL QUESTIONS

Of all the tools, your own analysis of your financial situation is probably the greatest one because it comes from your own inner wisdom. Let's apply the "best and worst" method to instantly determine outcomes. Make a list of the things that you want to purchase. Now answer the following questions: "What's the best possible outcome from buying this piece of land, home, dress, boat, etc?" and "What's the worst possible outcome that can happen from this purchase?" The five minutes you spend on answering those two critical questions honestly will add joy to your life – by saving you from potential problems down the road.

THE ESSENCE OF THE BEST

I believe in the winning concept of communication when dealing with money. This is controversial because our bureaucratic system is based on win-lose methods. In the book *No Contest*, Alfie Kohn states that "our fates are linked in that I cannot succeed unless you fail. Thus I regard you as someone over whom to triumph."

Kohn further discusses the concept of cooperation, believing that the success of each participant is linked to that of every other. The structure leads to mutual assistance and support, and helps cooperators feel an affinity for one another.

In winning negotiations, the needs of the two parties are aligned. The attorney who wants fair settlements already has the desire to create the fair financial agreement. The consultant who wants his client to increase sales will want to give winning sales strategies to the client. And the real estate broker who is concerned with the need of the client to find the right property will spend the proper amount of time doing the research, so that he or she can meet the financial and emotional needs of the client.

The next step is to turn this into a negotiation. The key to negotiation is *desire*. Both parties must have a strong desire to make the deal happen. Emotion and desire play a large part in financial negotiations. The problem is there are often emotional issues underneath the financial ones. Remember, money alone is neutral. The representation of love, power, or prestige, represented by the symbol of money, is what creates many such powerful reactions.

There is a way to deal with the emotions before the negotiation that will save you emotional and physical wear and tear. The following are preventive measures for freeing up the often stuck negotiation process.

Questions To Ask

- What is it that you really want besides the possession that this money will buy?
- What do you feel is the fair price for this item?
- Why are you negotiating? What bothers you about the price as it stands?
- Why is it too high or too low?
- If you could create the ideal situation around this negotiation, what would it look like?
- If you could create the ideal situation for both parties, what would it look like?
- Which situation feels better to you, the negotiation where you win or the negotiation where both parties win?

What I have found to be increasingly true in our culture is that lack of money is so often associated with low achievement and low self-esteem. Abundance of money is often associated with high achievement and a feeling of high self- esteem.

We all know that the amount of hours you work, the profession you choose, and the actual number of dollars you produce, has *nothing* to do with your worth and value as a person. Yet, the underlying message pervading our society is quite the opposite. Not paying bills, not being able to buy the gifts you desire, not having the things that you feel you deserve, not being able to participate in activities with friends, not having the financial ability to buy instead of rent, all conjure up feelings of failure, laziness, and lack of self-esteem. We have to pay attention to our feelings about the lack of money and get to the root of them, as the following chart demonstrates.

Money Action	Feeling	Value
Buying Clothes	Enhanced appearance	Self-Esteem
Owning a home	Being protected	Power
Owning a business	Making personal impact	Power
Having bills paid	Responsible, clean	honesty, truth
Buying a Special Dream Present for yourself	Pampered Self-sufficient	Self-love
Goint on the Vacation you choose	Rewarded Excitement	Freedom
Taking your family out to dinner	Care-Giver "tooth-fairy"	Self-worth
Buying an equipment toy - such as a VCR, car phone Stereo sound system.	Enjoyment Ease	Self-love

In analyzing the above chart, the feelings and values attached to money become much easier to understand.

Those values of self-love, self-respect, freedom, honesty, and power are at the root of our belief system and are the keys that open our hearts and ignite our motivation.

The major question then becomes what to do with those feelings about money that trigger such basic values? How do we make peace with ourselves and our situations and keep our values intact? I would like to explore each of the values mentioned in the table and develop positive "money" scenarios around each one.

SELF-ESTEEM AND SELF-WORTH

Self-esteem and self-worth are the backbone of our emotional life, just as the spine is the backbone of our physical life. Without the spine, we lay powerless, unable to use our strength. Without self-esteem and self-worth, we also lay powerless, unable to use our strength. When money is associated with the core of our existence, it becomes easy to understand why we often feel stripped of value.

Dilemma: Lack of money, lack of self-esteem and self- worth.
Positive Action: Surround yourself in wealthy, supportive environments where you feel rich, strong and valued.

Examples:
- Ask for the gift of a lavish meal in a lavish restaurant.
- Volunteer to be part of the opera, ballet, or symphony activities.
- Spend time with loving, kind people who have "made it" and value you as a total equal.
- List your greatest achievement which *gave you a feeling of total self-worth that money did not buy.*

POWER
Power is another strong value that all of us crave at

least once in our lives. For many, power is a constant passion that drives them with tremendous force. In their positive forms, money and power can do much for others. Many philanthropists have been the source for cures for disease, built foundations, and made vast contributions to the environment. In their negative forms, money and power have created sickness, death, and destruction.

Dilemma: Lack of money and power.
Positive Action: Find new activities to generate money and positive power

Examples:
- Work on positive charitable projects.
- Counsel others with your expertise.
- Find a financially and personally rewarding project.
- Visualize yourself with power and its relationship to the money you want or need. Turn the visual image into a reality.

SELF-EXPRESSION
Self-expression typifies creative individuals, like writers, painters, or actors. Such individuals always make unique contributions to our culture. How does self-expression relate to money? Only to the extent that the creative person is hampered by a lack of tools he needs.

Dilemma: Lack of money and inability to express the self.
Positive Action: Find financial resources that support your means of expression

Examples:
- Begin networking to find people who support your work, finding ways to help them and yourself toward your goals.
- Work for an artist where you can do your artwork while helping the owner promote his work.

- Sell the products or services you believe in that will place you in contact with more people who share your values.
- Exchange your creative energies for exactly what you need (a painting for printing services, a marketing consultation for brochure design, sales contacts for media advertising space).
- Write a proposal for your ideas or turn your creative gifts into a form that can be appreciated by the public.
- Write a book about your ideas.
- Sell your hand-made crafts at fairs or shopping malls.
- Sell your entrepreneurial idea to a backer who can see the monetary rewards.

These financial resources may be long-term projects, but the effort will keep your creative energies moving.

HONESTY AND TRUTH

Most of us give lip service to being honest, but few of us adhere to the simplicity of the value. Again, our society does not support telling the total truth and, in some cases, white lies and partial truths are for the good of the situation. However, it is important for us to understand and know what our personal truth is and what is absolutely true for us to live by, work by, and aspire toward.

Honesty is an integral part of money. When we feel dishonest about money, it may mean we are afraid to buy things for which we cannot pay.

Dilemma: Lack of money.
Positive Action: Tell yourself the truth about your financial situation

***Things To Do*:**
- Call your creditors and work out a payment plan.

- Purchase something you have wanted for a long time that you can comfortably pay for in installments.
- Write a few sentences about what you want, need, and see yourself having.

**Nothing is too big
If you can see and believe it**

FREEDOM

Freedom and money go hand in hand, taking advantage of opportunities and allowing creativity to take place. Pursuing a career, buying a business, traveling to explore new business opportunities, or producing your own video, all require capital. When money is not available, it may hamper our dreams and hold us back. Here are ways to work through this problem.

Dilemma: Lack of money causing constriction of action.

Positive Action: Assess the times you were "free" and act as you did during those times.

Examples:
- Create what you want on paper.
- Freely express your ideas to colleagues.
- Borrow money, or work to create the finances you need.
- Do something that makes you feel free, like walking in the woods.

The more you practice freedom, the more it will become part of you and bring the money you need for your ideas.

SELF-LOVE

Self-love seems easy. After all, we know ourselves, and share feelings of love for others. Why, then, is it so difficult to transfer those feelings of love to ourselves? Self-love is misinterpreted as being selfish. Love of self may exclude others, but not necessarily.

When we care about ourselves, we can care more for others. You can't give something you don't have within yourself. Money is a good way to express wants and desires, and you don't have to spend a lot of money to feel good.

Dilemma: Lack of money causes feelings of deprivation.

Positive Action: Use money to nurture and pamper yourself.

Example:
- Treat yourself to a special dinner every two weeks.
- Buy yourself a bouquet of flowers which makes you feel good.
- Listen to sensual music that soothes you.
- Treat yourself to a massage or a new hair style.

Taking care of yourself fills up your well so you can continue your life's work, putting energy and money back into the system.

8

Networking

*T*his chapter is designed to inspire you to develop tools on which to build networks. My own business was built in this way. I found networking fun, easy, and a great way to make new friends. Here are some systematic ways to network.

CHOOSING THE RIGHT NETWORKS

There are two types of networks – one for personal growth and one for professional growth. Search for organizations in your area which will promote each of these two important areas. It is also valuable to join state and national organizations in your field, where you can learn new state-of-the-art techniques to enhance your business.

The following tips are for selecting networks:

1. Do your research. Learn where the networks are located. Many are listed in the Appendix of this book.
2. Join national networks for general information, publications, newsletters, and conferences.
3. Join local networks for business contacts and associations.
4. The best connections come from the referral of friends. Tell your friends what you need. The right contact may be closer than you think.

5. Participate in activities based on personal interests. It's easy to meet people when you are doing what you love. Many business deals have been initiated on the golf course or at parties.

6. Help other people. Become a source of information for others. This will put you into the hub of activity.

7. Go out to lunch with a new acquaintance in your field. You can give each other valuable information, new ideas, and new resources.

8. Use reference books from the library. Listings of companies, institutions, publications, descriptions of products, statistics, and countless other pertinent information are already at your fingertips. Don't reinvent the wheel. (See Appendix)

9. Use the power of the written word. Write articles, books, newsletters. These will leverage your position by reaching many people from one source.

10. Target and focus. There are thousands of networks. You could be meeting people forever, but you must have clear vision. Without clear goals, you will be left frustrated and scattered. Know what you want, so you can find it.

MAZE THEORY OF NETWORKING

I call this the maze theory because the process looks just like a maze when it's charted on paper. I learned this system about five years ago when I had the opportunity to use my skills as an executive recruiter. I worked for a search firm where my primary responsibility was to find candidates for specialized corporate positions. I was left with resource guides, reference directories, the telephone, and my personality.

In looking for the right candidates, I would call company departments to find out who worked in the specific position I was targeting. I would then tell that person what I needed, to see if they might have an associate or friend looking for a position. This is an effective method because people always know others in their field and sometimes they are looking for new opportunities. It is important to be honest in your requests and tell the person what you need. It is up to them to offer information. The following is an application of the maze theory.

FINDING A BACKER
1. Choose a point of contact. Go to the library. Find the reference book that lists venture capital sources. Find your local association or group.
2. Go to a venture capital meeting. There, you will meet investors, bankers, accountants, and other professionals in the financial services area.
3. Talk to someone at the meeting who will listen to your ideas. Get the name of the contact.
4. Go back to the office and call the referral. Use the name of the person from the meeting. Make this an exploratory call. State your idea in a general manner and listen for other ideas. Try to get more names.
5. Call the next name and use the last person's name as a reference.
6. Call as many people as necessary until you speak with someone who sounds and feels like a match.
7. Set up an appointment to meet that person.

The maze consists of the number of contacts you make that seem to lead to the next corridor. Getting through the maze depends a lot on your own personal tenacity and stamina.

COMPUTER NETWORKS
There are many computer generated data bases that can be assessed by a few key strokes and the telephone lines. You exchange information among computer users and tasks are delegated, to increase efficient use of time and resources. For example, a newsletter can be composed by a person in computer unit A, who then sends the

information to the graphics person in computer unit B, who then sends the updated material to the layout person in computer unit C, who then sends the completed document to the printer computer unit D. At any point in the chain, the document can be routed in reverse for corrections or additions as needed.

A national electronic bulletin board is like a big networking party of electronic information. Here everyone can interact with other computer users having a clearinghouse for their ideas. In a global sense, your office can then become the entire country through computer link-ups. The only difference between an office computer network and a national electronic bulletin board network is a matter of size.

FRIENDS AND NETWORKS

We often confuse our friends with our networks, and there is a fine line between the two. It's true that we can make key business contacts through our friends, and it's also true that we can jeopardize a good friendship if we overextend our requests. The following are suggestions for enhancing our friendships and making contacts:

1. If you know that your good friend knows someone you would like to meet, discuss your ideas with your friend and then ask, "I would love to meet X. Do you think it would be appropriate for you to make the introduction for me?" Be sure to tell your friend that the friendship is more important to you and that you only want them to make the contact if they feel comfortable.
2. When you make the contact, initially refer to your friend. After that, you are on your own. The consequences of the meeting and further interaction should never involve your friend. Your friend opened the door. That's all you asked for and that's all you should expect.
3. If your friend knows this contact well, you can cer-

tainly discuss your meetings, but only to get advise on your project.

Successful results begin with getting in the door. Our friends can provide the magic keys to opening doors, if we see them as magical and treat them with the utmost respect.

NETWORKING PARTIES

Whoever said that you should not combine business and pleasure did not know about networking parties. I recently had a networking birthday party with two other people who had similar birthdays. We had the party on a Sunday afternoon, sent out flyers stating that it was a networking party and to bring food instead of presents. About seventy-five people came to the party. We introduced each other, made new friends and business acquaintances, and had a great time.

You can create your own networking parties without a lot of effort. Find a group with similar interests and attitudes and invite them over. Ask the people you invite to bring a good friend who would enjoy this type of party. Request that your guests bring food, so that you can make the planning easier on yourself. This is such a wonderful way to meet new people and share ideas.

Business networking parties usually occur at holiday time. Christmas parties are a good example of sharing friendship, light conversation, and good times with colleagues from the workplace. Networking can take many forms, but, at its best, it allows us the opportunity to learn, enjoy, and make new friends.

LEVERAGE AND NETWORKING

We discussed leverage in the chapter on money. Leverage can be the most effective result of networking. The more people you meet, the more the word of your work is received by the public. Leverage is created by you, whether it's from media, publications, newsletters, advertising, or public speaking. You are the one who makes those networking decisions.

When you think of leverage, think of reaching the greatest number of people. Individual referrals are important, but there are other ways to make contacts that will increase your networking leverage.

Local organizations will increase your leverage locally by introducing you to many potential clients and customers in your area. We all need local clients to support our community, even if our business is on a national level. Through your participation in local events and promotions, you can get a sense of the community's support and resources.

National organizations provide a different type of leverage. Here you have the opportunity to connect with the leaders in your field. Those people are a great source of information and may be part of other networks applicable to your work.

Trade shows are a tremendous source of "networking leverage" because the numbers of people attending can range from two thousand to twenty thousand, depending on the topic and geographic area of the trade show.

The best way to decide which organizations to join and which trade shows to attend is to make careful selections based on your needs.

PERSONAL NETWORKING STORIES

The John Travis Story

The following is a story to illustrate the long-term benefits of networking. Several years ago, I attended a seminar in Boston, conducted by John Travis, author of *The Wellness Workbook*. John is a medical doctor from California and one of the pioneers in the field. I used his book and, before long, I began to send him written critiques from students in my classes.

Three years later, I brought John to the Whole Life

Expo in New York City to conduct another workshop. Our friendship developed and, with it, an invisible network was forming.

Two years after the second workshop, John called to ask if I would like to join a network of people in the health field. I attended the meeting, and met an incredible group of people with whom I now stay in contact.

The point of this networking story is that I maintained my goals and kept special contacts over the years, not knowing how the network would grow. These situations are unique because a special bonding takes place which can lead to lifelong associations. It is exciting to have personal and professional goals blended with other people who are on your "wave length."

The most meaningful networks are created when you follow your life's purpose and path.

The Sophia Tarila Story
This story combines intuition and initiative. One of my friends is a publisher and called to tell me of a national publishers' conference in New York. I knew I had to attend in order to make contact with the presenter, but what I didn't know was that the right contact was listed in the presenters portfolio. The contact is Sophia Tarila, publisher of *New Marketing Opportunities, Vol. I & II.* I was excited to learn about her marketing workshops and that she lived in Sedona, Arizona, where I was planning to visit.

I was happy to have found a colleague and I rushed home to call Sophia. We corresponded and talked for several months and sent material to each other. She sponsored a workshop I conducted in Sedona and she later came to Connecticut and New York, where we conducted joint workshops. It was an opportunity for me to become part of a major network and meet a new colleague. What was even better, I listened to my inner voice and it worked.

The Judith Mahrer Story

I noticed a business listing one day, in a national holistic networking catalogue. I called the founder of the *Connecting Link* in Denver, Judith Mahrer, and, through her resources, my business accelerated to a great degree. I have kept the connection with her and she is a good friend as well. In this case, I could combine my values, my work, and my social relationships.

VENTURE CAPITAL GROUP MEETINGS

I attended meetings of this group in Boston several years ago. The organization meets in many different areas of the United States. People are categorized into venture capitalists, founders of start-up companies, management personnel, and service providers. Each person had one minute in which to explain their professional wants and needs. Then there is a guest lecturer, followed by social interaction. Many business deals were created at the Venture Capital meetings. It was fascinating to meet such ambitious and bright entrepreneurs.

The Appendix contains an extensive list of networking tools to enhance your success.

9

Phone Conversations That Work

*T*he telephone is one of the most powerful means of communication ever developed. Communicating by phone is much different than personal confrontation. Fifty-five percent of all interaction with people is done through body language, thirty-eight percent through tone of voice, and seven percent with words. This means that when you use the phone, your communication skills rely on your auditory and kinesthetic senses, since your visual skills are not available to you.

FEELING WORDS

We feel a tone evoked by the words we hear. This sensation is very apparent during phone conversations. The content is less important than the tone which conveys the message. If the tone is inconsistent with the words, the listener may get a different opinion of what you are really saying. Pay close attention to the feelings you experience in response to the words you hear.

The following is a list of statements and feelings people receive, depending on how the sentence is delivered.

1. *I haven't heard from you in a while.*
This sentence could mean: I am angry that you haven't followed up on our previous discussion;
Or it could mean: I have missed hearing from you.

2. *I don't want to sign this agreement.*
This could mean: I don't want to sign this agreement, but I do want to close the deal;
Or it could mean: I don't think this agreement is fair and you haven't represented me well.

3. *I have to discuss this matter with my boss.*
This could mean: I agree with you, but I need approval;
Or it could mean: I don't agree with you and I want to discourage any further discussion on this issue.

4. *I need a shipment in the mail immediately.*
This could mean: You have been ignoring my requests;
Or it could mean: I am happy with our business relationship and there is urgency to my request.

It is in these examples that the tone conveys the real message. The listener must interpret the meaning. If you feel confused, be sure to ask the person to clarify what they are saying. When you say you have to discuss this matter with your boss, does this mean you don't approve of the issue or he might not approve of it?
Pay attention to the emotional state of the message. Develop and refine your sensory awareness. Work on "phone intuition."

USING THE QPN MODEL ON THE PHONE
The key to strong positive phone communication is your ability to deliver concise, clear and direct messages. Here you can apply the QPN Model to your conversations. The tone of your client may help you

discover new needs on his part. Once the needs are determined, the Q must be evaluated to help you choose qualities appropriate to the needs of the client at that time. If he or she is angry, listening skills and empathy are needed. If he or she is confused, you can become more direct and help to organize his thoughts and ideas to clearly demonstrate the qualities you have to offer.

It is important to continually check and make sure that your purpose (your needs and desires) match those of the client. For example, things may be proceeding smoothly until your client changes his mind in a way that contradicts your values, beliefs, and common sense. It is time to check in with your (P) purpose to see if it still matches the client's (N) needs. If you have your purpose clearly in mind, you will be able to immediately recognize the disparity and decide how you want to handle the situation. Paying attention to your feelings as you listen to the client's words and tone will help you determine if your purpose is still in alignment with his needs. Having the QPN Model in front of you before the phone conversation will enable you to use it at a moment's notice.

CLEAR PHONE MESSAGES

Once you have a clear picture of your purpose in relationship to client needs, you can then begin to construct and deliver a clear and concise phone message. Answering the following questions will help develop clear messages:

1. What is the point of my message? Can I deliver the point in less than one minute?
2. Has my client or customer understood my messages thus far?
3. What new points are important for me to communicate to the other party?
4. Have I written down my points and can I recite them in a spontaneous way?
5. Have I left clear and concise messages when I can

not speak directly to the other party?

The answers should be filled out after the yes or no response. This material will help ease any anxiety or fear in dealing with clients over the phone.

THE SECRETARY-LINK TO YOUR SUCCESS

The secretary is a strong link in communicating with the manager or executive. Upper-level management, and corporate officers, usually have secretaries who have been assigned, or have taken on, the role of protector, mentor, and organizer. The personal secretary often knows as much or more about the executive's schedule as he does. Befriending the secretary and confiding in him or her with your situation or problem can often bring results that you might not get on your own. This is not manipulation; it's the necessary process of getting to your destination. The secretary has been hired specifically to screen calls. When it is understood what you have to offer, he or she can help you get through.

Suggestions for befriending the secretary:

1. Ask the secretary's opinion about your idea.
2. Ask for suggestions on exactly how to approach her boss.
3. Show your sincere interest in the company, and your respect for the busy schedule of the executive.
4. If possible, take the secretary to lunch.
5. Write a thank-you note, or call to thank the secretary for help and encouragement.

About five years ago, I sought a position as a business skills trainer for a major consulting firm. I explained my position to the secretary and got to know her well, before I even met the director. When I finally met him, he congratulated me on my persistence in trying to get an appointment, and enrolled me in a week-long training program so I could become an instructor. I could not have created that opportunity without the support of the secretary.

When the secretary asks the nature of your business, always have a ready answer. You want to be connected with the right person. The role of executive or manager varies from company to company, and what might be the duties of the Vice President of Human Resources in one company may be handled by an officer in a different department in another company. Many times I have called asking for the Director of Marketing, when I should have spoken to the Director of Public Relations or the Director of Personnel.

COINCIDENTAL DIRECT CONNECTIONS

Sometimes fate really works in your favor. This is true when you have done your inner homework. Here are two stories to illustrate perfect phone call timing.

Several years ago, I wanted to be affiliated with IBM. I had written and produced a television program that I felt might fit into their outstanding communications department. I lived near their corporate headquarters, so I decided to go right to the top. I called the main number and asked for the secretary's help to get me to the right person. She rang the Communications Department and "coincidentally" the vice president answered the phone. I was so surprised, I can't remember what I said, but I believe I communicated well. After five minutes on the phone with him, he said to me, "Well, it sounds like you should come in and talk with some of our people. My secretary will call to set up an appointment." I was happily amazed. Before I knew it, I found myself at the doorstep of the IBM corporate headquarters.

I spent three hours with the directors of media and video production sharing my tapes and talking. Although there wasn't a match for me at IBM, I made a connection with the Director of Media and went to see him two years later. I still call him from time to time to ask for information, advice, and to give him an update on my work.

The next scenario was created by a friend, Joan-Ellen Foyder, a consultant in the health care field and author of *Family Caregiver's Guide*, which assists those helping their ailing family members at home. She had designed a promotional kit for the health care consumer and wanted to market it to an international health care products manufacturer.

Joan-Ellen called the company and told the secretary that she needed help reaching the person who was primarily responsible for a particular consumer education product. Her first words to the secretary were, "I really need your help." After the secretary responded, Joan-Ellen said, "You sound like just the person who can help me." The secretary asked Joan-Ellen to hold while she tried to get some information. She gave Joan-Ellen the name of the Senior Vice-President of Marketing.

Joan-Ellen dialed the number, expecting to speak with the personal secretary of the vice-president, but, to her unexpected delight, she reached the senior man himself. Using the QPN Model, Joan-Ellen delivered her message succinctly. She made a point of telling the vice-president how much she appreciated their product and the company's accomplishments in providing information to the public. She then went on to explain that her kit would extend the promotion of their product.

The vice-president listened carefully to her description, which showed him how her product would meet the needs of the company. He asked her to send all the information about the kits. When she followed up with a phone call to make sure that he received the material, he set up an appointment to meet with her. Joan-Ellen took a financial risk because the corporation was 1200 miles away. She told the vice-president that she was going to be in the area. The risk of buying the airline tickets paid off, because Joan-Ellen found herself in front of the Board of Directors.

Joan-Ellen did all the right things. Prior to the phone

call, she readied herself with a personalized mini-script, which outlined her prime selling points to interest this particular company. Once she reached the right person, she utilized her script to thoroughly explain the value of her kit and how her product would benefit the company. She followed up immediately by sending the information and calling the vice-president within a short period of time. Once Joan-Ellen had the opportunity to present herself in front of the Board, she was able to use personal qualities that matched the values of the group.

These stories are not luck, but represent the gift of perfect timing. Yet, timing alone cannot produce results. Individuals must know their own visions and goals and be able to deliver that information at a moment's notice.

HANDLING TOUGH PHONE QUESTIONS

How can you answer tough phone questions with poise and grace? What if you do reach the "key" person directly. What do you do next? This is where your inner homework pays off. Hopefully you can respond quickly and easily. Here are some points to help you:

Question 1: "What is the purpose of your call?"
This tells you the person at the other end does not want wasted words – so get to the point. *Response*: Should be direct. You must quickly explain why what you are asking would benefit the other party.

Question 2: "What is your background?" *Response*: I am a consultant and writer with extensive background in sales and psychology. I have designed a skills program which I have successfully implemented in several major corporations that will motivate employees, thereby increasing productivity.

Question 3: "Are you assuming that I am interested in your idea?"
This tells you that you have oversold your idea and it

is now time to change the focus to the customer while addressing their issue. *Response*: I apologize if I have appeared to be overzealous. I believe in this product (or idea), have seen it work, and sometimes get carried away in my enthusiasm. However, you did mention that there has been low morale in your department over the past few months, and I know that this program can help your employees. I would be glad to send you my proposal and testimonial letters from other companies who have endorsed the program.

Question 4: "Do you have data to support what you are saying?"

This question implies a skeptical attitude about your service or product. Here you must have some facts to establish credibility. If you have the facts, you must be able to get them to the person. If you don't have the facts, you must be able to show in some way that what you have to offer will provide the results you are describing. *Response*: I can send you a brochure which explains my service and indicates results other clients have noticed.

GETTING YOUR MESSAGE ACROSS

When you are selling on the phone, you have only a certain length of time in which to get your message across. Try to be sensitive to the time constraints of the other party, and keep your message to a minimum if necessary. You will know when you and the other party are on common ground, or if they have time for a long or short message. The initial phone call is usually brief because it is a door opener to test interest in your product or service. Once you have created interest, the next step is to back up your ideas with facts and send out all pertinent material, such as brochures, articles, or tapes. By sending out this material, you are automatically creating a reason to make the follow-up call. It is advisable to call back within a short period of time to find out whether your material has been received. During this next conversation you have the opportunity to find out at what level the person has developed an interest in your material, what their organizational needs are, and if they have any objections. This is a critical call, because here you begin to meet the needs of the client. Developing rapport over the phone creates a bonding and trust which will facilitate your first in-person meeting with the client.

The phone creates a particular advantage when distance is a factor. However, it can become a limiting factor during the critical points of negotiation, when a personal meeting makes the voice and issues come alive. An example to illustrate this point comes from a friend who had a long-distance business relationship with her attorney. The lawyer was handling her property settlement from five hundred miles away. They had met several times, spoken on the phone at great length, and sent documents back and forth. But, eventually, when the documents needed discussion before the signatures could make them final, my friend flew out to meet with her attorney. Seeing the papers, facial expressions and gestures made the difference in closing this case.

NOT GETTING THROUGH

There are times when we say the right words in the initial phone conversation, send out our material, and make the follow-up calls, and still can't get through to the right person. This is when I again call upon the secretary for help. When you present your case with facts and clarity, many times the secretary will give you assistance.

My own story will illustrate this point. About three years ago, I called the publisher of a major publication to discuss a possible affiliation with the magazine. The secretary advised me to write a detailed letter, which I did. I must have spent three hours composing the letter and sending my material.

I waited what seemed to be the appropriate amount of time and then made my follow-up call to the publisher. I was told that he was in a meeting and not available. This

happened at least three more times. On my next call, I
said to the secretary, "I was advised to write to Mr. X,
which I did. I have called at least three times. He has not
returned my calls." I went on to say, "I spent several hours
compiling my material for Mr. X, and I would appreciate
the courtesy of his responding to my letter." She listened
carefully and said, "I know exactly what you mean. I'll
make sure that he gets this message."

Within three hours, Mr. X called me back. He had received and reviewed my materials. Although there was
not a match at that time, he discussed the scope, needs,
and direction of his publication with me.

The following telephone tips will help you get through
to the right person:

1. Make sure that you have taken all the necessary
   steps up to this point: initial call, mailings, follow-
   up calls.
2. Space your return phone calls and make a note of
   them with the date, so that you can track them with
   the secretary.
3. Always ask the secretary when you should call back
   and when the person you are trying to reach is most
   available. List times such as early morning, the
   noon hour, or late in the day. If you are dealing
   with a corporate executive or store owner, there is
   usually a time pattern that he or she follows. Try to
   set an appointment to call at a convenient time.
4. If you have called several times, ask the secretary if
   he or she can discuss your issue with the boss and if
   you can meet with him in person. Make sure that
   the secretary understands your product and service
   before you ask him or her to speak on your behalf.
   This is not the best strategy. It is to your advantage
   to meet with the person directly because you know
   how to promote yourself and your product or service. However, if that opportunity is not available

to you, ask for help from the secretary who can then pass on the information.

5. Last, but not least, try to put subtle pressure on the person through the secretary. It worked in my case, but I can't guarantee it will work every time.

THE PAYOFF OF PHONE PERSISTENCE

How many times have your phone calls not been returned by those people with whom you have established warm, professional relationships? And how many times have you given up after the second or third try, writing the person off as uninterested and uncaring? I have had so much success with people whom I have gently persisted calling. The success came from my belief that we had a positive relationship. I have left messages for salespeople, business consultants, and physicians with whom I was working, only to find out, after I finally reached them, that they were out of town, extremely busy, or didn't get my message. And those people, "because they were the right connections," came through for me in their intentions and agreements. Since this has happened so often, I have come to the following conclusion: Persistence pays off when you follow your intuition. I would change the adage "if it's worth having, it's worth fighting for," to "if it's worth having, it's worth persisting for."

UNIVERSAL INTERVENTION

However, there are times when you don't reach that person, even after gentle persistence. I believe that when I have exhausted all possibilities, and have not reached the person by phone, there is a universal message here. The message is that I wasn't supposed to reach the party. You may feel this is a rationalization or a "sour grapes" attitude. I have consistently found that the more "on purpose" I am, the more often the right opportunities either don't present themselves at all or they fall by the wayside. And I have learned that as long as I stay true to my beliefs, "right action" will happen.

TUNING IN TO PHONE MESSAGES

Phone intuition is valuable when listening to messages on an answering machine. These messages give one an opportunity to digest the information, listen to the tone, and sense the feelings of the caller. It also gives time to assess your own feelings in relationship to the message. Ask yourself, "What is the real message behind the words? What does the voice tone and speed of delivery tell me?" Phone answering machines are effective when:

1. You want to screen calls.
2. You want to leave your message so it will be heard without immediate feedback.
3. You don't want to miss important calls.
4. You need additional time to tune in to your own feelings.

In a live conversation, one needs more skill to tune in. You need to let your inner guidance let you hear the message.   Instead of blocking yourself, you begin to hear words and register your feelings. Eventually, you can listen and understand two conversations at once, theirs and yours.

CREATING PHONE BUSINESS

Today the phone is the prime tool for business of all kinds. This is especially true in the case of selling products or services. Here is a checklist to use when placing phone orders, that focuses on the product and the feelings of the person on the other end of the line:

1. Tell the person exactly what you need.
2. Make sure they understand.
3. Give them an opportunity to explain about an upgraded product.
4. Ask them to repeat numbers to you.
5. Check shipping and delivery dates and write them down.
6. Get information about new products that interest you.

7. Make sure you have the name of the person taking your order.
8. Make note of the person's tone and attitude.
9. Keep a log of your phone conversation, so that you will have a record of your business transaction.

Having your purpose, ideas, and questions on paper keeps you on track and in line with your vision.

PHONE USE AND ABUSE

The phone is a very powerful tool, but it can easily fall prey to abuse. A key distinction between phone use and phone abuse is that phone use accomplishes a purpose, whereas phone abuse drains your energy. Some indicators that you can use to help you identify phone *abuse* are:

- A constant and insatiable yearning for more words, more ideas, more dialogue;
- Continual talking to a client or potential client who remains noncommittal and seems to have endless objections;
- A person who often calls you and talks for long periods of time about personal problems or business-related issues – but never seems to move toward completion;
- Having no boundaries by allowing the phone to interrupt meetings or work sessions;
- Excessive and continuous personal calls during work hours.

If you notice any of these symptoms, you can take the following assertive action to eliminate them.

- Set limits with your friends. Let them know you are serious about your business and have set aside certain hours for working. Then stick to those hours and arrange to call back at another time;
- Allow your answering machine to screen calls;

- Ask your secretary not to interrupt you during meetings or work sessions;
- If you do take a call during a meeting or work session, explain that you would like to talk with the person, but you are in a meeting. Set an appointment to call back;
- Keep personal conversations short and set aside time to meet with friends;
- Check out reasons for allowing the phone to interfere with getting your work done. You may have fears that are keeping you from accomplishing what you want to accomplish. Identifying fears can help you become more effective on the phone. If it's a persistent problem, consider seeking professional help.

It is true that, without the phone, many of your professional and personal relationships would be severed because of distance. However, it is up to you to be aware of the "real hook" that the phone has on you. If abused, the phone can create a mechanism that supports addictive behavior and relationships. If used properly, the phone can increase and enhance your business relationships.

This is certainly the case with the car phone. The car phone can be a handy "tranquilizer" when in a traffic jam, lost, or late. It can also become the catalyst for accidents. The car phone can be an essential success factor for the salesperson, executive, or entrepreneur. In the car, calls tend to be shorter and more to the point than in your office. I totally support the car phone if it is used correctly.

The phone can be one of your greatest success tools. Learn to use it effectively. Remember, you control your ties to the phone. Don't let the phone lines tie up your life.

10

Communication Skills

C ommunication skills are the essence of success in both life and business because they are the manner in which we convey ideas to other people. This chapter contains specific communication skills I have used over the years, and which have worked for me.

I-MESSAGES

Years ago, when I was teaching parenting skills, I taught a concept from Thomas Gordon's *Parent Effectiveness Training and Leader Effectiveness Training* called the concept of "I" messages and "You" messages. The "you" message is a direct attack on the other party involved. Examples of "you" messages are:

"You didn't type that correctly."
"You were late for the job."
"You are not listening to my idea."
"You are not scheduling your time well."

The "I" message is the message which states and expresses your feeling as the sender of the communication. Examples of "I" messages are:

"When you are late, I feel the job isn't getting done."

"When you ignore the schedule, I feel that you don't respect the rules."
"John, I am concerned, because your constant phone calls are not producing results for the company."

Instead of blaming the person, you should examine and express your own feelings. This method has helped me on many occasions and now I send "I" messages automatically. You can practice this by saying the words "I feel" before you begin to say "You did" or "You said." Beginning your sentence with "I feel" reduces the risk of the other person feeling that they are being attacked. By using the words "I feel," you are addressing the specific behavior of the person and not blaming the person. Your feelings belong to you and no one can argue with them.

THE SKI SLOPE

I was coming down a beginner's ski slope when someone rushed by me, almost knocking down our entire party. I quickly said, "We are beginners on this slope and your fast skiing almost knocked us over. I wonder if you could move to the more advanced slope?" This was far better than getting angry. The person quietly moved away and we were not bothered again. The point is that I didn't use an attacking statement, but appealed to the person's logic and reason.

NEUROLINGUISTIC PROGRAMMING (NLP)

Neurolinguistic Programming, NLP, invented by Richard Bandler and John Grinder in the 1970s, is the study of how verbal and nonverbal language can be used to program our nervous systems. NLP shows us how to communicate with ourselves and understand how other people communicate. We communicate through our five senses: auditory, visual, kinesthetic, olfactory, and gustatory.

In *Unlimited Power*, Anthony Robbins describes how we use our Visual, Auditory and Kinesthetic (VAK) senses. People who are primarily visual tend to see the world in pictures. They achieve their greatest sense of power by tapping into the visual part of their brain. Because they are trying to keep up with the pictures in their brain, visual people tend to speak quickly. People who are auditory tend to be more selective about the words they use; they have more resonant voices, and their speech is slower, more rhythmic and more measured. People who are kinesthetic tend to react even slower, primarily to feelings. Their voices tend to be deep and their words ooze out slowly. Everyone has elements of all three modes, but most people have one system that dominates.

By understanding the communication modalities of clients, it is easier to develop rapport with them. If I deal with a client who talks rapidly and seems to create pictures for me (visual), I respond accordingly. By speaking very slowly, needing a concrete example to hold on to (kinesthetic), I would present a conflicting sense. Clients will respond best to someone using the modality most familiar to them.

When you are speaking on the telephone, you are primarily relying on your kinesthetic sense for feeling the energy and your auditory sense for listening to tone. However, the person you are speaking to may communicate in a visual mode. Pitch, tone, and speed are clues which determine the modality of communication each person uses.

Using the NLP techniques, I "pick up" on the energy of my clients and try to copy the patterns they use. This is not a ploy to manipulate people, but rather an attempt to harmonize our communication by speaking the same language.

One of my clients is visual, a quick thinker, and a person who wants concise information. She appreciates my speedy delivery. Another client is more kinesthetic and I once had to slow down my delivery because she said I was going too fast. Thus, I changed my approach with the two clients, making them feel more comfortable with the conversation and how the information was delivered.

The senses can play a part in enhancing our professional growth. Some people pick up information through a variety of senses. Regardless of the sense you use, the information may be valid. We all associate certain smells and tastes with certain people or events. This is quite normal. Thus, you can utilize the sense that is most familiar to you.

WORD POWER

Words are powerful. Thoughts are things, and these things become translated into the pictures you create with your words. Your beliefs and attitudes are transmitted through your vocabulary. Achievers use success words like "I can, I will, of course, yes," and "I know." Those words create a positive feeling, just as the words "I can't, I won't, I shouldn't, I forgot," and "I'm awful" create a negative self-fulfilling prophecy.

The following are examples of positive word power with your clients:

"Sure, I can do that for you."
"I'll give it a try."
"We will find ways to make this product adapt to your situation.
"I will look at a creative way of financing."
"I support your idea."

Our words create pictures for our clients and we need to choose them carefully. If I tell my client that something is small, it could mean minuscule, tiny, or almost medium. Big could mean large, enormous, or gigantic. And nice could mean pleasant, pretty, well-designed, or well-decorated. The more descriptive the words you use, the clearer pictures you will be able to draw for your clients and customers.

COMMUNICATIONS

We discussed winning negotiations in the chapter on

money. It is important that both parties share in this experience and have the freedom to express their ideas. Even if the other person doesn't agree with you, it is beneficial to walk away with the feeling that one is understood. Tesa Albert Warschaw, in her book *Winning by Negotiation*, discusses that each party must be willing to give up a certain amount in order to achieve winning negotiations. This involves an appreciation of differences and an acknowledgment of other people's viewpoints.

POWER LETTERS

Letters make a very strong impact on certain people because words have permanence. The written statement tells the story without debate and it tells you that the writer means business. In many cases, I have seen the content of letters change when the people meet face to face, but the written word makes the initial impact. The QPN Model can be applied to the following types of letters:

The Inquiry Letter is a subtle solicitation about your service or product. It applies when you are looking for a position, want to submit an article, or are introducing yourself. The QPN Model applies here. State your qualities and your previous experience, and any other pertinent data.

The Appreciation Letter sends thanks and gratitude. It can be used after a meeting, after a phone conversation, or any other encounter with clients. Writing this type of letter shows appreciation and committment.

The Resume Letter is a historical document that expands points of your resume. It tells who you are and what your goals are in more detail. It can be a letter to an executive, someone to which you have been referred, targeted companies, or future clients.

TURNING A MISUNDERSTANDING INTO WINNING

I was searching for a candidate to fill a corporate position when I worked at a personnel agency. I called someone I knew who had offered to promote my work, but I had turned down her gracious offer. When I phoned her that day, she answered abruptly, and it was clear she didn't want to speak with me. Because the relationship mattered to me, I mustered up the courage to call her back. I said, "I felt distant from you in our conversation.   Have I offended you?" She said, "Well, I wanted to help you in your business, but you turned me down.   You dropped me like a hot potato." Her words shocked me. I had no idea I had rejected her. I said, "I'm so sorry.   I didn't realize what I had done. I was concerned about my budget." She answered, "Well, you could have told me that, and I would have taken partial payments.   I was really hurt." I apologized and this opened up the lines of communication again.

The incident taught me a lesson. As Richard Bach says, "We teach others what we need to learn for ourselves." I felt courageous in calling her back, but the relationship was important to me. When two people can express their feelings and resolve differences, they both feel empowered.

You can't change other people or make them respond the way you want. You can only change yourself and decide if you want to maintain relationships with difficult clients. If negativity brings out the negative part of you, suggest that a colleague handle the account. You must love and respect your own boundaries, and live by them.

THE TRADE SHOW

I coordinated a trade show for an organization and accepted the opportunity with no salary in exchange for a workshop presentation and advertising. As my work on the project progressed, I began to feel cheated because the amount of time and effort I was putting into the project far exceeded my return. In addition, the producer of the trade show was extremely judgemental and her favorite method of communication was to win by intimidation.

One morning, I called her at home to inform her that I couldn't finish the work without additional staff support.

Her first comment was, "How dare you call me on a Sunday morning when I need to sleep? There's never enough for you. Every time you call me you always want more." I listened to the anger behind her explanation, took a deep breath, waited for a pause in her tirade, and said, "Joan, I understand your position. I know that you have given me many thousands of dollars worth of publicity and public relations and that the exhibitors and speakers are paying you for what you are giving me. I appreciate that. But I want you to know that I generate as much income from giving my lectures. This is a special project that I agreed to become involved in, but it has taken so much of my time that I have not been able to finish my income-producing work." I stated the facts, appealed to her reason and logic, and did not blame or criticize her or the organization. So, after she listened, she asked me what I needed and compensated me by hiring a secretary to finish the job.

I was dealing with a woman who "pushed my buttons." However, I was still able to communicate and make enough impact for her to change. Confronters who win by intimidating others can usually be neutralized by facts and evidence. Retaliating with words only adds fuel to the fire. And, as I grow and change, I watch myself relinquishing the win-lose relationships even if it means that I lose an opportunity. I now believe that a better opportunity is right around the corner, one in which I will attract the people who want to create winning relationships.

OPEN COMMUNICATION LINES

Good communication creates good relationships. We all want to be liked and understood, with relationships that work. Sometimes we perceive information based on our past. We build a communication monster. When communication is blocked, we must express our feelings to prevent the situation from getting worse. I compare open lines of communication to telephone lines. When the phone lines are down, no one gets through. When they

are open, we can reach our parties. Keeping your communication lines open comes from a desire to listen to the
other side, and works toward mutual understandings.

11

Time Management

W e must learn how to utilize our time. In a sense, time is like clay. Larry Dossey, a medical doctor, discusses man's internal clock, and the fact that we know what time it is on an internal level. We create our own inner clock, and thus the saying "Time is of the essence," is quite valid. I have rephrased that statement by saying, "The essence of who we are is part of our internal core."

HAVING CLEAR GOALS

How we use our time tells about our needs. Having clear goals acts as a road map and sets the direction we take. Our goals may change, just as we may take an alternate route when driving on the highway. Goals spur our actions. Without them, our actions would be diffused and scattered.

Sometimes our goals seem so large we think they are out of our reach. The key to goal setting is being able to see smaller goals within the context of the overall vision.

As each goal appears closer and has practicality in the here and now, it is easier to see action we can take based on that goal. Then we are motivated to move on to the next goal.

It is important to see all the components within the vision to make our dreams come true. We need to put our goals into a structure. People who complain they aren't accomplishing anything have not organized their time around a structured goal.

THE TOOLS OF TIME

The tools of time management include daily lists of things to be accomplished, weekly and monthly schedules, and yearly plans. I find that leather books, with places for notes, are very helpful. They allow me to organize my thoughts and ideas, and put them into a time structure. The major advantage of this system is that all dates, times, and goals are accessible in one convenient place. It allows one the opportunity to see progress each week or month. I have listed several time management systems in the Appendix.

Another way to prioritize activities is to use index cards. Each goal is listed on a card and the activities that actualize the goal are itemized on the card. This activity can also be done on the goal page of the time management book. Seeing the list of activities is a way of breaking down the task into "sizable chunks" or steps. Because it sometimes seems too obvious to write down our activities and lists of things to do, many of us keep ideas and facts in our head. Making lists and composing ideas on paper is a habit that is developed solely from the practice of doing it. Written statements are intentions that become commitments. Even if we change our ideas and plans, the written lists remind us where we have been and show us why we chose that goal or activity at that particular time.

The key ingredient to successfully reaching your goals is that your activities reflect them. I feel that about eighty percent of our activities should be related to our purpose. For example, if your purpose is to help others achieve and maintain a sense of wellness and half of your time is spent playing tennis, the most sophisticated time management system in the world will not help you manage your time. The time management tools you choose are only useful to clarify your goals and activities.

Keep Organized

Here are things you can do to set things straight.

1. Keep your desk free of papers.
2. Organize material by subject and importance.
3. Prioritize the workload.
4. Get extra help.
5. Train other people to understand your system.
6. Create a schedule for another employee.
7. Schedule uninterrupted time in which to do your work.

Motivation means desire – desire to fulfill our goals and dreams. Passion is the driving force of motivation. Tapping into your passion means paying attention to your real desires. Then work and joy become interchangable – and the essential ingredients to timely success.

THE DELICATE TIME BALANCE

There are times when we cannot stay on track with our goals. We want to follow through, but time pushes us further away. We are distracted from the task at hand. It is important to blend work with diversion. Balance is the key to determining how this blend will occur and balance is the state of being many of us strive for and struggle to achieve.

Assessing how you spend your time is the first place to look in trying to balance your life. And having clear priorities is the key to achieving balance.

I recently read a story about a successful corporate president who stayed in touch with his family by wearing a beeper. This showed his commitment to his family by being accessible to them by phone when he couldn't be there in person.

Each of us has different family and work goals, but it is important to know how much time you give to the different parts of your life. Having those commitments on paper will help you stay in a balanced position. It's easy to get off course with all of the distractions in any one day, but, if you understand the reason for the interruption, you can begin to deal with it. In cases where the same interruption occurs continuously, it is important to work through the underlying causes for the disruptions.

I spend a lot of time making business calls and cultivating friendships. I also make a fair amount of personal calls, always trying to balance the professional with the personal. When I track my calls, it helps balance my time, and I am more efficient.

CREATIVE WAITING TIME

We live in a society that rewards doers. The more we accomplish, the smarter, richer, and better we are. This notion has made time our most sought after commodity. Those of us who can accomplish goals in the shortest amount of time become role models. Our sports figures are timed on performance, as well as being given recognition for their particular skill. Living one day at a time, and completing tasks with excellence, are touted by the experts. It is often difficult to apply this principle because the patience it takes to wait for results often ends up in frustration and anger.

Patience is a virtue and it can help us reach our goals. Waiting time is when new ideas and possibilities take root in our minds. When we constantly run and do, there is no space left to develop intuition. New inspirations stay locked in the subconscious and only appear when we "crash" from overload.

Patience can be a catalyst for creative thinking while the universal clock does its job. The universe has its own time schedule and when we heed that schedule, new doors open. We can speed up the time clock by visualizing exactly what we need so that we can attract the right opportunities. When I needed a public relations person, I simply "asked" for one in my subconscious mind and the right person appeared to help me with promotion.

Waiting time is really germinating time, where "the seeds we have sowed are growing and developing." We reap benefits when we receive the positive phone calls from clients and colleagues.   Waiting time is creative learning time and an important investment in our future success.

LEVERAGE AND TIME MANAGEMENT

The most successful people master their use of time. The more we use leverage, the more we accomplish by not always "doing." Leverage is a good time manager. The following are examples of time leverage:

1. Having a secretary collate and staple all your material. This saves you hours of time and let's you increase your income by doing more important activities.
2. Hiring a public relations consultant to get you on radio and television programs because the consultant has instant connections. This can save you weeks and months of time.
3. Having a cleaning service clean your office, so that you can spend the time developing new clients.
4. Having all your lists on a computer diskette, so that you can find names in seconds instead of hours.
5. Having calls screened so that you can focus your time.
6. Hiring a bookkeeper to keep track of your expenses.

I compare time leverage to flying instead of walking. Although I discussed leverage in the chapter on networks, I feel it is important to discuss it from the point of view of time. Since we operate in linear time, the rate of speed that information travels greatly affects our position and results.

Time Leverage: A way to "expand" time by increasing the number of people you reach in a given period of time.

THE QPN MODEL AND TIME MANAGEMENT

By knowing your purpose (P) and the needs (N) of the client, you can being to estimate the amount of time it will take to deal with a particular issue. And if your qualities and purpose match the needs of your client, you can speed up the process by pre-determining the outcome.

In the following example, time management is illustrated by using the QPN Model.

The patient tells the physician she has an ailment and wants to be treated with a specific medication (N). The physician feels that the patient needs a complete physical examination (P) and, although he explains the reasons in detail (Q), the patient refuses (N). The physician uses professional ethics (P) and refers the patient to another doctor. Instead of "fixing the patient's ailment (N)," and running the risk of a future complaint resulting in the expenditure of time and money, the physician stays true to his own purpose (P).

Sometimes the best time management tool is letting go. Those of us who try to fix all the clients who pass through our doors are operating under the assumption that we can be all things to all people. Some clients just have to be released in order to give space for the productive client relationships to come into our lives.

TIME LIFESAVERS

Fifteen minutes of daily planning can be worth a full day's work. Spending a few minutes on the following points will save time and revitalize your energy:

1. Read your goals daily.
2. Write your "to do" list at the end of each day.
3. Check off the most important items in the morning.
4. Eliminate the rest of the items for the day.

5. Take time for relaxation.
6. Exercise to release stress.
7. Speak to a friend who supports you.

I have named the preceding items "time lifesavers" because they "buy" clarity and focus. Being clear makes the difference in getting to our destination. By writing down the items, I feel as though I have accomplished them and that "they are as good as done."

As I put the words on paper, my commitment in writing helps me make the commitment to myself.

TIME DRAINERS
Some items drain our time and energy. They are:

1. Fretting over what you can't change.
2. Phone calls that appear useless.
3. Arguing to no avail.
4. Doing errands someone else can do.
5. Worrying about the future.
6. Piling up papers, instead of filing them.

The fifteen minute negative call can cause two hours of frustration. Piling instead of filing costs hours of search time. If this is happening to you, it is time to take action.

UNDERSTANDING PRIORITIES
Our goals are formed from our visions, and the priorities are the activities and actions derived from our goals. We choose priorities based on what is most important to us both personally and professionally. However, managing priorities can be a difficult task. For example, exercise is a priority for many of us. Although this doesn't seem to relate directly to one's work, it increases one's energy level, which directly affects success. Priorities often consist of mundane tasks that will manifest long-term results, like filling out forms for degrees, licenses, and permits.

Determining priorities is always contingent upon our needs. Urgency develops when there is a threat of losing what we want and need. Our "time urgencies" become our "life urgencies." A good barometer to use in determining a priority is to ask yourself, "Why is this important? What's the urgency? Does it have to be done today?" Then stand back, and answer the questions from a detached point of view. Many times, what we think are urgent "to-do's" can really wait, as illustrated in the following example.

Betty is a real estate broker trying to close a deal within two weeks. She must speak to the attorney before the deal closes, and she can't seem to reach him. She is worried about the delay. However, a two or three day delay will not affect the transaction. Because of Betty's personal issues, she spends a good part of the day worrying that she has not been able to reach the lawyer.

In this case, emotion plays a large part in determining priorities. What we think is a priority may really be part of an internal fear that the outcome will not occur.

TIMING DISTRACTIONS

Distractions encourage procrastination. They happen even when the distraction is an enjoyable part of our lives. I am often distracted by helping friends, cleaning house, calling airlines, filing, and other unimportant tasks. This often happens when I should have concentrated on more important issues. Here are ways to deal with necessary distractions:

1. Get help doing routine tasks.
2. Focus on major priorities and set time limits in which to accomplish them.
3. Reframe your thinking so that distractions become rewards, instead of "necessary" distractions.
4. Make a list of distractions and choose the ones you like and don't like.

We should enjoy positive distractions and get rid of the negative ones. We use a considerable amount of energy worrying and feeling guilty. We should transform that energy into more important tasks so we can preserve our vitality and self-esteem.

THE REWARDS OF TIME

The following are ways to evaluate time spent:

1. List five healthy activities in which you have engaged over the past six months.
2. Examine your time management system for the past month and note your achievements.
3. Reflect on the positive feedback you have received at work.
4. Look at the major goals you have achieved. See the distance you have traveled instead of the miles left to go.

Time is our most precious commodity. It gives us many options. We can use it to "beat ourselves up" or appreciate where we are and where we are going.

12

Creating Balance – The Body Mind Connection

I t is interesting that stress management is such a hot topic today. So many of us take on "everything," instead of "some things," and we walk the tightrope of time, always living with the threat of falling off. We seem to lack the one simple ingredient that would change it all – *balance*.

THE ISSUE OF BALANCE

In response to the pressures of work, difficult people, and win-lose situations, it's easy to swing to the extreme side of the pendulum. The result is compulsive behavior about work, food, alcohol, sex, and spending. There is a way to catch these behaviors, before they deteriorate. Prevention is the focus of this chapter.

Believe it or not, rituals can actually help to keep you on steady ground. For example, clearing your desk at the end of the day, saying good morning to each of your staff members, exercising and having meals at a certain time each day, and spending time in daily meditation are habits that create positive structure in your life. When the daily exercises become compulsive behavior, habits turn into

117

obsessive rituals. These compulsive and obsessive behaviors create enormous stress in our bodies and move us away from a state of health and balance.

The following chart shows examples and results of extreme and balanced behavior:

Extreme	Result	Balanced	Result
13 hour work days	Exhaustion, Competency reduced, *Ulcers*	8 hour work days	Energy restored through action plan
50 phone calls a day	Saturation, "Burn-out", *Neck pain*	25 phone calls per day	Client satisfaction
Strong negative reactions to staff complaints	Loss of communication, Reduced productivity, *Depression*	Listening to staff complaints before acting	Open communication, Enhanced productivity
Adhering to rigid time frames	Exclusion, Isolation, *Hypertension*	Flexible time frames	Team work

Heal Your Body, by Louise Hay, connects mental causes to physical ailments. Power-packed with explanations of particular physical complaints, the book is worth reading for its fascinating philosophy. Hay states, "We have learned that for every effect in our lives, there is a thought pattern that precedes and maintains it . . . This new awareness brought me understanding of the connection between thoughts and the different parts of the body and physical problems."

REFRAMING OUR THINKING

We can prevent many of our physical problems by becoming aware of the thought patterns that contribute to them. Our negative self-talk, and our negative visual images, are fuel for the thought pattern. In order to change the thought pattern, we must change the words and pictures we have been using to keep the thought pattern in place. Those pictures trigger certain feelings that are registered in our bodies, affecting the way our bodies feel. Reframing our thinking means putting a new frame around an old thought. And this new, positive frame creates a new positive set of feelings that are internalized in our bodies. The following are examples of stressors – situations that trigger the stress reaction.

Example 1.

STRESSOR: Traffic jam.

THOUGHT: I can't stand it. I'm missing an important appointment.

PHYSICAL SENSATION: Pain in pit of stomach.

REFRAME: There is nothing I can do about this at this moment. The client will understand when I call. I'll use the time productively and finish my report.

Example 2.

STRESSOR: A peer has embarrassed me.

THOUGHT: I want to kill her – how can she do this to me?

PHYSICAL SENSATION: Headache.

REFRAME: I'm embarrassed, but people know her behavior is inappropriate.

The reframe is more powerful when each sentence is repeated and visualized.

STRESS ON THE JOB

Stress is exploding in the workplace. A noted expert on stress, Hans Selye, explains that stress causes adaptations in the body to bring it back to normalcy, just as primitive man had the "flight or fight" response. Today, in our plush offices, we'd like to flee, but can't. So stress is produced inside our bodies.

However, there is an opposite side of the "stress coin." Eustress, or positive stress, is what we feel before meetings, interviews and special events. The outcomes are often exciting, challenging and positive, but they increase the demands on our bodies.

In a *Newsweek* article, April 25, 1988, it was indicated that stress costs the economy almost $150 billion a year, almost the size of the federal deficit. Now, many companies design stress management programs. The National Wellness Association in Stevens Point, Wisconsin produces a national newsletter, directory and conferences.

THE BODY DOESN'T LIE

Here is an exercise showing the relationship between body and mind, and how the mind influences well-being.

1. A volunteer from the audience stands in front of the group.
2. I ask the person to extend one arm out to the side, parallel to the floor.
3. Next, I instruct the person to close his or her eyes and visualize a wonderful and joyful experience.
4. When the person has registered the positive experience, I tell him or her that I will try to push down the arm and that he or she must try to resist.
5. The exercise is repeated again with the person visualizing upsetting or negative experiences.
6. I try to push the arm down again.

Results: In almost all of the cases, the person's resistance is weakened and the arm comes down easily. When positive thoughts are uttered, the arm usually stays up. This illustrates the relationship between body and mind, an exercise which is measurable and immediate.

THE CONCEPT OF WELLNESS

I have been involved with the wellness movement for ten years and it has benefitted my attitude, behavior, and health.

My favorite book on the subject of wellness is *Wellness Workbook*, by John Travis, M.D., and Regina Sara Ryan, which I introduced as the text for a teachers' course several years ago. *Wellness Workbook*, which gives clear examples and provides readers with an experience into the state of well-being, defines wellness:

"Wellness is never a static state . . . Nor is wellness simply an absence of disease. While people often lack physical symptoms, they may still be bored, depressed, tense, anxious, or generally unhappy with their lives. These emotional states often set the stage for physical disease through the lowering of the body's resistance . . . Wellness extends the definition of health to encompass a process of awareness, education, and growth."

For me, wellness has been a process of respecting and appreciating my needs on a physical, mental, and spiritual level. It has meant an understanding and awareness of what is going on around me, for all of it is interrelated. Your workplace and the people in it can affect you. In the following examples, try to recall your feelings at work and how these situations affected you:

- crowded elevator to your office;
- smiling face of your secretary;
- the constant complaints of co-workers;
- the telephone call to your favorite client;
- the papers stacked on your desk;
- the surprise flowers from a new client.

All of these affect you physically and mentally, setting the tone for your work day. Even one of the items can create a strong impact and "make or break" your day. Positive thinking can be your lifesaver. It has a stronger force than any other kind of energy, and can dissipate negativity in your environment.

The environment sets the stage for workdays. If you are constantly bombarded by negative forces around you, note the difference in how you feel. Are you in pain or fearful? Or do you feel warmth, joy, and ease? Positive statements make you feel good. When you feel good, your body doesn't complain. Try to monitor the number of negative statements you make.

We can choose to ignore the signals and information that our body transmits to us. But if we listen, and respect those feelings, we elect to move toward a state of wellness in our lives.

YOUR WORKING DIET

Have you ever wondered why you get sleepy after business lunches, become irritable right before lunch, or crave caffeine and sugar to keep you going?

These physical reactions are signals from your body that it is out of balance in some way. Nutritional choices affect our state of mind. Creating nutritional balance is directly related to creating balance in our attitudes and moods.

The following suggestions for good eating are taken from *Wellness Workbook*:

1. Increase consumption of fruits and vegetables and whole grains.
2. Decrease consumption of meat and increase consumption of poultry and fish.
3. Decrease consumption of foods high in fat and partially substitute polyunsaturated far for saturated fat.
4. Substitute nonfat milk for homogenized milk.
5. Decrease consumption of butterfat, eggs, and other high cholesterol sources.
6. Decrease consumption of sugar and foods high in sugar content.

7. Decrease consumption of salt and foods high in salt content.
8. There is strong evidence that caffeine has addictive properties and contributes to erratic blood sugar levels. Coffee, black teas, colas, and chocolate, which are all high in caffeine, should be taken with caution.
9. Since many urban water supplies are contaminated with toxic pollutants such as lead, asbestos, and mercury, consider using bottled spring water or attaching a high-quality filter to your spigot.

Following these basic recommendations will affect your performance at work. Reducing or eliminating coffee in the morning contributes to the reduction of mood swings and nervousness. Heavy business lunches increase the blood supply to the gastrointestinal system, making blood less available for the brain. Eating foods rich in water (fruits and vegetables), and easy to digest, will increase your efficiency and enhance your problem solving ability. I often use the phrase, "Eat for lightness," by which I mean to eat to feel light mentally, physically, and spiritually. Annemarie Colbin, founder of the Natural Gourmet Cookery School in New York City and author of *Food and Healing*, discusses the theories behind food and how to find the right balance for your body by eating natural foods. I highly recommend her work and cookbooks as ways of bringing balance into your life through nutrition.

THE BENEFITS OF EXERCISE

Exercise shapes our bodies. But it also shapes our minds. When we exercise, endorphines are released in the brain, producing a tranquilizer-like effect that helps reduce anxiety and tension. Other benefits of exercise are increased energy and stamina, reduced fatigue, improved circulation, fewer body aches and pains, increased resistance to disease, improved self-esteem, and healthier lifestyle preferences.

Three major types of exercise are aerobics, flexible exercises, and strength developing exercises. Here's how you can add movement to your day:

1. Use stairs instead of elevators.
2. Hand deliver memos.
3. Take a walk at lunch.
4. Take breaks once an hour.
5. Do stretching exercises during break time.
6. Park your car several blocks away from the office and walk.

All of these movements add up to a healthy total. They will become automatic if you keep them in practice.

LIFESAVER OF LAUGHTER

Laughter is a powerful form of healing. Physiologically, laughter deepens beathing, strengthens the immune system and massages the internal organs. Laughter offers a form of detachment and reflief from our own situations.

Laughter also stimulates the thymus gland which protects the immune system, becoming a source of illness prevention. Among the benefits of laughter are:

- Stimulating deep breathing;
- Helping to "save face" and deal with difficult people;
- Bringing a new perspective of "lightness" into the matter;
- Transforming bad moods; and
- Adding joy and fun to our lives.

THE BREATH OF LIFE

The key to relaxation can be summed up in one word: *breathe*. We all know that breath is a vital sign of life, and that its job is to supply energy to the bloodstream. Breathing is studied by singers, musicians, and yogis, but often overlooked by the rest of us. Breath is a key element, because oxygen taken into the lungs is the life force.

Most of the time we breath automatically and unconsciously. When we are aware of our breathing, we are temporarily distracted from issues. Breath is a powerful tool in dealing with confrontation. When you are asked uncomfortable questions, or bombarded with information, you can simply stop, and breathe deeply. By consciously inhaling a large supply of oxygen, your body pauses to "absorb it." A simple breathing exercise is to take in a large breath to a count of three, hold it for another count of three, and then release it to a count of three.

You can vary the amount of time you hold and release, but the idea is to give the body time to feel the new energy. Probably the most noted book on the subject is *The Relaxation Response* by Herbert Benson. There are many excellent books and tapes on the market that use sound, language and music to help you relax, increase motivation and self-esteem, facilitate learning and create and maintain balance. You can find a list of these resources in the Appendix.

THE JOYS OF MEDITATION

Meditation can bring you peace of mind and give you insights that only come from the meditative state. In *High Level Wellness*, Donald Ardell explains the effects of meditation:

"Meditation lowers the body's oxygen consumption, blood lactate level, carbon dioxide elimination, heart and respiration rates, fatty acids in the blood, and acts beneficially on other processes connected with the sympathetic nervous system. It also increases the likelihood and duration of alpha brain-wave cycles, and reduces muscle tension throughout the body. All this, of course, is just the reverse of the effects of the unattended (i.e., not acted upon) fight or flight response, so the importance of a quieting technique as a way to manage stress is apparent."

Since meditation quiets your mind, it allows you to listen to your intuition. The following is a list of meditation benefits:

1. Clearer choice about time allotments.
2. Greater ability to make personnel decisions.
3. Better focus with clients.
4. Staying with projects until finished.
5. Remaining true to your values.

Career transitions can also be a problem. One can bridge the gap by meditating at a solitary place, such as at the beach or in the woods or listening to guided meditation or submininal tapes. These will help you to begin to let new inner goals and visions surface. In these fertile environments, thoughts and feelings will grow and develop.

SELF AWARENESS AND RESPONSIBILITY

You can create balance in your life when you become aware that you have a responsibility for your choices. The following suggestions will help you:

1. Learn to trust your intuition, the voice within.
2. Allow for self-expression.
3. Learn about your stressors.
4. Make good nutritional choices.
5. Become aware of and act on your body's need for movement.
6. Enjoy the sensory awareness and pleasures of nature.

The way of wellness has provided me with a sense of balance through my major life transitions and changes.

13

Learning Lessons

*T*he reason that many of us give up before our dreams come true is that we allow ourselves to be stopped by our mistakes. A mistake becomes an obstacle, like a fallen log across our path and directly in our way. Our reaction is usually pain and frustration. The experience is then registered in our mental storehouse. Whenever we recall the memory or experience a similar situation, up comes the experience and its negative information.

These experiences become a protection and safeguard which can stop us from repeating the same mistakes over and over. Those who learn to make visions into realities are able to make mistakes, sift through them, and find valuable lessons.

A mistake is a valuable lesson. However, when we continually repeat mistakes, we strengthen the validity of our past experiences and maintain "old attitudes," which create a vicious cycle. In order to learn from our mistakes, an attitude shift must occur, allowing us to see the whole scene differently.

HIDDEN CLUES

When you try to view a scene differently, look for clues that made the experience a mistake in the first place. Generally speaking, before the mistake occurred, there was some hidden clue that you either didn't see or heed. The following examples are the types of mistakes people make in their professional lives. The corresponding clues, which, if recognized, would have averted or minimized the mistake:

MISTAKE: I took the job because I was attracted by the perks.

CLUE: In my excitement, I did not listen to the job description.

MISTAKE: I choose the wrong business partner,

CLUE: I did not check into the person's business history because I was so "grateful" to have found a "willing and able" partner.

MISTAKE: I allowed the company to pressure me into a relocation.

CLUE: I couldn't get excited about the new area to which I was moving.

MISTAKE: I did not get results from all the money I spent on promotion and advertising.

CLUE: I had doubts about the effectiveness of the material, but trusted the experts at the expense of my own intuition.

MISTAKE: I took the job because of financial necessity.

CLUE: I knew all along that the job would not encourage my creative growth.

MISTAKE: I wasted my time with innovative ideas that were never recognized by the company.

CLUE: The management kept saying that they would get back to me, but constantly stalled me.

EXAMPLE #1

Computers in Demand

Kathleen was a sales representative for a computer company and had many corporate clients. One of her client companies placed an order for several hundred computers. Kathleen knew that these computers were in demand, since there was a back up on the orders. However, she was so excited about the number of sales and the tremendous response that she overlooked a possible delay in shipment. Her client was waiting for the computers, and Kathleen, in her flurry of activities and constant movement on the road, did not let the client know of the delay. The client was angry when the company did not receive the order when promised and Kathleen almost lost the account.

MISTAKE: Kathleen did not set realistic goals with the clients.

CLUE: Kathleen knew that the shipments might be delayed, but didn't anticipate the time urgency of the client.

LESSON: When you set unrealistic goals, you "set yourself up" not to meet them.

AFFIRMATION – I communicate realistic time frames to my clients.

AFFIRMATION – I return phone calls from clients promptly and stay in frequent contact with them.

EXAMPLE #2
The Wrong Partner For Janice

Janice chose a partner, John, based on good rapport and the reputation of his past successes. The relationship worked well during the first year. However, John was often rude to clients and ruined the business' reputation. Eventually, Janice dissolved the relationship and found another partner.

MISTAKE: Janice chose the wrong partner. She should have known this, based on John's prior behavior with his secretary and his family.

CLUE: Janice saw this behavior in John's family interactions, long before she entered the partnership.

LESSON: When we focus attention to the surface of a situation, we don't see the internal problems.

AFFIRMATION – I choose and find a valuable partner whose personality and abilities complement my own.

EXAMPLE #3
Plunging Into The Stock Market

Ellen invested considerable money in the stock market, against the advise of her advisors. She worried about having her assets tied up, but decided to follow her own intuition. The market crashed and her stock fell dramatically. She lost thirty percent of her investment.

MISTAKE: Ellen felt let down by the market. She convinced herself not to take this type of financial risk again.

CLUE: Ellen sensed a change was coming in the market and was warned to do something to protect herself.

LESSON: When we make choices, we must know the risk clearly and accept the consequences.

AFFIRMATION – Life is a classroom. I see the results of my choices and accept the consequences toward a perfect ending.

AFFIRMATION – Money is an ebb and flow. As it is released, so it will flow again. I release the flow of money into my life and abundance will come.

EXAMPLE #4
The Administrative Stand

Eric was an administrator. He was extremely efficient as a manager and became proficient in scheduling and programming. He really enjoyed logistics and writing reports and was known for making and keeping deadlines. Yet, as the workload increased, Eric spent more time on administrative duties and less time on his staff. Eric was aware of the problem, yet he did little to change it. Eventually, the "people" part of his job was given to another staff member.

MISTAKE: Eric was aware of work preferences and would not admit them for fear of losing his job.

CLUE: Eric was rarely available to consult with his staff on an individual basis.

LESSON: When you try to cover up real desires, the truth always shows through.

AFFIRMATION – I focus on my strengths, do the work in the world that makes me happy, and achieve success.

EXAMPLE #5

The Mentor

Bill had known Ken for five years and had become Ken's mentor at work. Ken knew that Bill had a lot of friends, was close to the top people at the company, and Bill had listened to Ken and given him sound advice over the years. One day, Ken was called into the president's office and was questioned about certain methods and procedures that were not in strict accordance with the company. Bill was the only person Ken had talked to about his personal strategies and could have been the only person to have talked to top management. Ken felt betrayed and hurt.

MISTAKE: Ken chose the wrong mentor. Bill did not respect his confidence and it hurt Ken's reputation, status, and feelings. Ken swore he would never again confide in anyone at work.

CLUE: Bill often shared very confidential corporate issues and personal stories about other staff members with Ken, always telling Ken that no one else knew of them.

LESSON: When you give away your power, you give another person the right to control you.

AFFIRMATION – I trust my own inner wisdom to make the right choices.

AFFIRMATION – My past mentors provide wonderful examples to make appropriate choices in the future.

MISTAKES AND NEW GROWTH

Each mistake is like a scene in a play which we can play again, or choose to do differently in the future. Forgetfulness often precedes our mistakes because we are distracted and preoccupied by present or future thoughts. When we spend the time to learn the clues and lessons from our mistakes, we can then fill the vacuum with new positive experiences.

Look at your life. If you keep making the same mistakes, look at what you are really doing and play it on your mind screen. You must make a conscious effort to change. Awareness is not change. It's only a preliminary step. Watch for clues and see where you are headed. This permits you to learn from your mistakes, in order to move on in your personal and professional growth.

14

Overcoming Isolation

*I*t is easy to become motivated when you are doing what you love. The key to motivation is passion, but all business people occasionally get into a rut. Here's what you can do if this happens to you.

CHANGING YOUR MIND SET

Work overload, poor communication, the inability to express yourself, and fear of job loss all lead to feelings of isolation. Then we bury ourselves for protection. Isolation puts you face to face with your problems. The first step is to recognize you are a valuable human being and deserve to have the best opportunity in which to utilize your talents.

One of the laws of prosperity is that we attract what we are. If we feel isolated, we need to shift direction and make new choices. If we remain self-contained, we tend to close the circle around us and see everything from our own perspective. Eventually, the picture can get distorted.

Other people can bring you new perspectives and expand your points of view. When you are isolated in your office, the idea that people are unreceptive to your ideas becomes implanted in your mind.

By opening the door to other people, you are creating fertile ground to let new ideas come in. Isolation can be a positive tool if used as a refueling station. But it must be interspersed with the ideas of others.

The following are ways to relieve isolation:

1. Break out of the cycle on paper and express how you feel on paper.
2. Call a favorite client or customer who will "pick you up."
3. Sell your services to an interested second party.
4. Get out of your office for a while.
5. Go to a networking meeting or a social event.

HOMEBASED BUSINESS AND ISOLATION

Working out of your home helps create isolation. You become your own critic and boss, and can easily lose perspective about you own progress. You need someone to validate your work. This doesn't mean you can't validate yourself alone, but we all need the stimulation of others. The telephone can help you to create the network you need. My telephone network exists across the country and sometimes I meet my friends and colleagues in person months after I've met them on the telephone.

Here are some thoughts for people who work alone:

1. Join networking organizations.
2. Have lunch with people in your field.
3. Share ideas with clients.
4. Use the telephone more.
5. Find a mentor who will help you.

These ideas will help you to expand your ideas and business growth.

PROCRASTINATION

Psychology experts tell us that procrastination is rooted in the fear of success and the fear of failure. Success and failure can manifest themselves in the following ways:

> *Success*:   fear of being found out – that you're not credible; fear of keeping up once you've made it.
>
> *Failure*:   fear of being rejected; fear of losing position and status; fear of not being perfect.

Success and Failure: fear of being a target for criticism.

Procrastination can immobilize you and occurs when:

1. We don't like to do something.
2. The job is too hard.
3. We're afraid we might have to repeat the task.
4. We're afraid to struggle and subconsciously fear pleasure.
5. We're afraid of humiliation if we fail.

When you have an enormous project to complete, it can feel like starting the climb up a mountain. Here are some ways to prevent procrastination:

1. Take one step at a time.
2. Praise yourself when you finish a difficult task.
3. Set time limits to your work.
4. Get someone to help you.

The key to success is to have and hold onto your constant vision. When the internal vision and motivation is so strong, you will make it your business to find the help you need to overcome blocks and reach your goals.

EXAMPLE #1

Marty is a stockbroker who loves his work. However, there are some days when he can't seem to get into working. For the past two weeks, he has experienced failure and rejection. To overcome the problem, Marty can stop making sales calls for a short period of time; call a colleague who understands the problem; or go out on a sales call with someone in the office who is successful.

If none of the preceding steps work, Marty should examine his goals. It may be that he needs a change in his job situation.

EXAMPLE #2

Theresa is a graphics designer, working out of her home. She has trouble getting up on time in the morning and is distracted by personal problems in the house. She could hire a secretary to come in each day to get her started. She can be kinder to herself by getting the help she needs to do the job.

MOTIVATION AND CHANGE

Here are ways to recognize when you need change in your work:

1. You watch the clock.
2. You leave promptly at the end of the day.
3. You only do what the job description states.
4. You take extra long lunches.
5. You "tune out" your boss.
6. You daydream on the job.

LUNCH BREAK MOTIVATORS

1. Write down what you've already accomplished this morning.
2. Make a wish list and do something to move yourself in the direction of one of your wishes.
3. Buy yourself a present.
4. Go to lunch with a favorite friend.
5. Go for a walk and listen to a motivational talk on your portable cassette player.
6. Visit a museum or other place of local interest.
7. Do an aerobics class.

WHAT'S BEHIND MOTIVATION

What's behind the burning desire to succeed? Values tell the story. The goal of making money is an external value. Internal goals are recognition, self-worth, and personal pleasure. However, money is also attached to the latter traits.

Sometimes we see only the outer motivational signs. When we learn to recognize internal clues and understand our underlying motivation, it's much easier to make clear choices. For some, it is better to have a job that gives you recognition, rather than one that creates a lot of money. For others, money is the prime motivation. It all depends on what your values are – especially your internal motivators – because they will unleash your motivation.

Sure Fire Ways To Motivate Yourself
Here are some good ways to relight your fire:

1. Talk to people who believe in you and your work.
2. Get confirmation and letters of recommendation from people who recognize your ability.
3. Listen to motivational tapes or read motivational books. (See Appendix)
4. Approach people who are interested in what you do.
5. Take a break to do something different and enjoyable.
6. Use your intuition to figure out what is holding you down.
7. Help someone else who appreciates your work.

We create power when we help others. This power fuels our inner strength and from this inner strength we make our greatest contributions.

15

Personal Quirks

*I*f you have physical features that bother you, or emotional problems with which you need to deal, you can do something about them. You don't have to accept limits on yourself. If you lose a job, something will intervene. The universe abhors a vacuum and will fill it immediately with something that is for your wellbeing, if you can create the picture you want to fill this new space. If you don't have a vision, anything can come in, and usually does.

SELF-PERCEPTION

Your personal quirks are defined by your perception of yourself. What may be beautiful to one person may be distasteful to another. For example, one person's nose may become a point of distinction.

Every part of your body expresses itself as a part of you. Until you learn how to integrate all the features of your external self, your discomfort will be transmitted to the people around you. However, you can accept yourself and still be uncomfortable with your nose, legs, double chin. Altering those physical flaws can help you balance your body and harmonize the positive picture you have established.

At work, you can find ways to use your quirks to your advantage. Your nose, your body shape, or your personality can be benefits. You can also get advice on clothing and make-up to enhance your looks. Maintaining a positive image on the job will help you to feel better, as well as look better.

Balance is the magic word that transforms personal quirks. We must create a balance between how we look and how we feel.

PERSONAL FLAWS

Several years ago, I interviewed a lady who had scars over her entire body as the result of a childhood accident. She was remarkable, because this defect did not stop her from becoming successful. She wore shorts and sleeveless dresses and was unafraid of what people might think. Here was a woman who truly accepted herself, and her body, with enough confidence to leave a successful career, to get married, and raise a family.

I have a bright and confident friend who is a senior product development manager for a large company. She has a very husky voice because of nodules on her larynx. I once mentioned over dinner the deep quality of her voice. Her response was, "It gives me character." She accepts her voice as part of her uniqueness and enjoys herself.

One of my colleagues is a petite, four-foot-eight powerhouse. At a meeting I attended, she was so diminutive that I didn't notice her until she gave me some networking tips. The woman is a master at what she does. Later, when we met for lunch, she said she feels her size is an advantage because people remember her. She's a perfect example of "walking softly and carrying a big stick."

THE TRANSFORMED PATIENT

This is a story about how a surgical procedure changed the way a person performed on the job.

A gentleman came into a plastic surgeon's office requesting nose and chin surgery. He wanted to reduce the size of his huge nose and enhance the size of his receding chin. He gave the overall appearance of a man burdened by the world. He was five foot two inches tall, walked with a downward glance, spoke in a low voice, and never looked anyone straight in the eye as he talked. His surgery was successful and his chin and nose achieved balance appropriate to his face.

Six weeks after the procedure, the gentleman walked back into the office and the plastic surgeon did not recognize him.

"May I help you?" the doctor asked.

"I'm Mr. Jones, whom you operated on six weeks ago."

In total disbelief, the doctor inquired about the events since the operation.

Before him was a man standing upright and tall, with a positive countenance, looking straight into the doctor's eyes. In an assertive voice, he described how his company had promoted him to managerial status. Although most plastic surgery cases are not this dramatic, this particular patient made a complete transformation. The benefits definitely exceeded the usual expectations.

QUIRKS

Quirks are part of life. Some of us are forgetful, others are scattered in their approach, still others are fast thinkers, or are compulsive in their behavior.

I once heard a story about an adolescent boy who came to this country and did not know the language. He also stuttered. The boy became a fine public speaker. He told his audience about his success in fluent, flawless speech. Here was a person who overcame a major obstacle in order to become successful.

UNFORESEEN CIRCUMSTANCES

Webster's definition of the word synchronize is "to happen or take place at the same time or instant." Synchronicity means things that take place at the same time. The stronger we believe things will happen for our highest good, the easier it is for these events to take place. I believe there are no coincidences, even though events may seem synchronistic.

Here are some examples:

1. John is delayed by a storm that caused a meeting to be cancelled. His presentation wasn't ready anyway for the earlier meeting.
2. Construction is delayed on a new office. The manager has to find another space and it is better than the first one.
3. The vice president of marketing is stuck making a difficult decision. He "just happens" to encounter someone at a meeting who helps him.

These happenings were not coincidental. They were the result of synchronicity and were for the greater good of the people concerned.

UNFORESEEN DELAYS
A delay is a gift of time. For example, Helen lost a job to another candidate. The other person decided against the position. A month later, Helen was called and offered the job.

Harold was in a traffic jam. It gave him time to prepare for the next day's meeting.

Bill had to wait for a client. He used the time to help clarify his thoughts before the meeting.

CREATING NEW OPPORTUNITIES
Here are ways to use your inner resources to respond to shifts in circumstances:

1. You lose your job. A new opportunity arises.
2. You lose a sale. This gives you time to prospect for new clients.
3. You lose communication with a client. It gives you

time to review the situation.
4. You are cramped in new, smaller quarters. It gives you a chance to clean out and discard old records.
5. You lose a business partner. You have time to reflect on what kind of a partner you really want.
6. A key employee resigns. This gives you a chance to regroup, re-evaluate and find the right new person for the job.
7. You are on the board of directors and urgent issues keep the board in session for extra days. You are behind in your work at the office. This gives your secretary a chance to excel, and you time to sort out top priorities.

THE GIFT OF UNFORESEEN CIRCUMSTANCE
The following may be gifts in disguise:
Computer Failure.
A car breaking down on the way to work.
Telephone lines going dead.
If the above situations, or others like them, seem to paralyze you into inaction, you can gain strength by knowing how to use your inner resources to deal with such events. There are many possibilities and alternatives to unexpected circumstances that can be turned into a gain for you.

LOSS TURNED TO GAIN
A typist I hired informed me she couldn't work for me anymore. I was crushed and took her leaving as a setback, somehow believing I would never find anyone who could do the job as well as she did. Then a friend told me about a typist who was available. As it turned out, she gave me all the time I needed to complete the project, and her skills were as good, if not better, than the other typist.

AGAINST ALL ODDS
Everyone has heard stories of people who dared the odds and made it. They had vision, determination, and

faith, putting aside circumstances to go for their goals. I have met people in business who turned flaws into assets. Anyone with determination can put aside problems and reach unbelievable goals.

Part of the process of reaching your dream involves going over bumps along the road. When you learn to deal with obstacles and not let them stand in your way, it is proof that you are holding on to the vision of your dream. Unforeseen circumstances test your faith and trust. They give you a perspective of where you are, and offer new alternatives. If you're on the right path, unforeseen circumstances will keep you there.

16

The Media Maze

*T*he media offers many ways in which to gain exposure and credibility. It provides instant leverage because of the large number of people it reaches.

RADIO AND TELEVISION

Start With Radio

Radio shows usually offer guest speakers more time to present their views than television shows. Radio shows allow you to express your feelings and deliver the message. When the visual element is eliminated, you can concentrate on expressing yourself without worrying about your appearance.

Call-in shows are radio shows that allow listeners to call the station with specific questions or arguments. They measure audience response and sharpen your ability to think quickly. Questions asked by listeners are good indications of the needs of the general public. Sometimes, you can return to the same show and address areas you did not have time to cover initially.

Television Talk Shows

Becoming a guest on a television talk show requires effort. Major network shows are more difficult to be booked on because they have a set format and are filled

145

with people who have specific information on their topic. It's always a good idea to call the producers and discuss the needs of the program before you send your press kit.

Television adds visual dimension to your presentation. Thus, hairstyle and clothing are as important as the interview. Your presentation will be maximized by clothing that suits you.

Getting On Media Talk Shows

1. Locate *Bacon's Publicity Checker* at your local library.
2. Call advertising agencies in your city for lists of stations.
3. Familiarize yourself with shows before approaching them with your presentation.
4. Call the producer or program coordinator at the station. It can be difficult to reach producers, so the more prepared you are the easier it will be to get your message across. Discuss your expertise in relation to their programming needs.
5. Call friends who have recently been on a program to give you the name of the producer and/or interviewer.

Producers are always looking for good guests and local programs are a great way to start using the media. Being on a show will build your confidence, credibility, and exposure. For the most part, local radio and television talk shows do not pay, but it's a great way to get free publicity.

Whether your interview is on television or radio, bring a blank tape with you and ask the studio technicians for a copy of the program. Or you can ask someone to tape the program at home, but you'll lose some of the quality. The audio or video tape becomes an important part of your professional portfolio.

Your Media Interview

On smaller shows, the host may also be the producer. This person coordinates the program, chooses the guests, and decides on the topics to be discussed. The following will help you effectively plan your interview:

1. Before you meet with the interviewer, know your purpose and the program needs.
2. Have a pre-interview with the producer.
3. During the interview, listen carefully to the questions.
4. You may add something to the program, but be sure to ask the host if you may do so.

Be well prepared. If you are put on the defensive, know how to respond. Don't worry about the audience. They can sense the dynamics of the show, especially if the host is sarcastic or manipulative.

Follow-up is the key to returning to the program. Many times, a producer or host will tell you they want you to come back. However, unless you're a best-selling author, or a prominent personality, the ball is in your court. It's up to you to send a note thanking them for the opportunity to be on the program, stating that you appreciate their offer to be on the show again, and letting them know that you'll call within a certain period of time.

Having been a guest on numerous programs and hosting my own shows have been wonderful growth opportunities, giving me a new perspective on my career. The media provides an opportunity to evaluate our growth as individuals.

THE POWER OF PRINT MEDIA

Print media gives you exposure by spreading the word to many people at once. It is very powerful because you can retain it for long periods of time. You can also absorb it at your own pace and in your own time and place.

Here are ways to effectively utilize print media:

1. Research the marketplace to see where your topic fits.
2. Don't underestimate small publications. They can give you a start.
3. Write a query letter to the magazine to find out if they are interested in what you have to say.
4. Follow up with phone calls after a reasonable time.
5. Call the editor directly to discuss his needs.
6. Write a follow-up letter if appropriate.
7. Send your article according to the magazine's specifications.

If you can reach the editor, he or she can motivate you. They may not be able to use your idea at that particular time, but may be interested in your work in the future. You may also find that one idea leads to another. The key is to be adaptable and remember that nothing is cast in concrete. Editors will work with you if they feel your concept has appeal.

Using the QPN Model to match your purpose to the needs of the editor will help build rapport and create a future working relationship.

ARTICLES WRITTEN BY THE MEDIA

You can find writers and reporters in the following ways:

1. Know the publication and their deadlines.
2. Find reporters in your specific department and learn if there is an interest in your material.
3. Go to meetings where colleagues can give you names of helpful reporters.
4. Attend publishing and writing conferences where you will meet people from the media.

Publicity Myth:
"No publicity is bad publicity" is a misnomer.

**Negative publicity is not good publicity.
It transmits negative messages and negative energy.**

SELF-ESTEEM AND THE MEDIA

The different facets of your personality are brought out by the various personalities and forms of the media. What you hear on radio, see on television, or read about yourself in print, is a part of you that has been seen through someone else's perspective. It may or may not agree with yours.

I've seen so many people stop before they even try to contact producers and reporters, because they were sure their work would not be accepted. Many times, a reporter is looking for an unusual topic or new ideas on a subject.

Here are some affirmations you can say to build self-confidence when using the media:

"I believe in my idea."

"My idea deserves the greatest exposure."

"This program is the vehicle that expresses my idea to the public in the best possible light.

These affirmations will help you focus on the idea instead of your ego. Once you are "outside of yourself," the fear of rejection and humiliation stays outside you.

FIVE KEY POINTS ABOUT MEDIA PEOPLE

1. They are just like you and me.
2. They need to meet the needs of their publication or program.
3. They are good resource people.
4. They are on the lookout for new ideas.
5. They are under deadlines.

There are many wonderful people in the media. Remember – in media relations, as in all other relations, you will get back exactly what you give.

17

Advertising
That Works

*P*ersonality enters into the way we respond to advertising. A risk taker might use the yellow pages. A cautious person might call friends for a referral. Intuition also plays a large part in the decision making process.

THE BEST METHOD OF ADVERTISING

I frequently ask colleagues and clients about the best method of advertising. Answers differ, depending on the preference of the person and their service or product. However, the best method of having people find out about you is word of mouth. It is also the least expensive.

The best way to use the word of mouth approach is through contacting many people at one time, such as:

- attending networking meetings;
- giving free lectures or talks;
- attending trade shows;
- publishing articles in journals from your field.

All of these are public forums where you work can be seen.

PLANNING YOUR ADVERTISING

Because advertising requires careful word selection, description and cost information, its very nature compels you to define and structure your business. Advertising dollars must be carefully spent to get the best return on your investment. Budgets vary according to a number of factors but publications, large or small, must be scrutinized before the money is spent.

Advertising spreads your word, but it must reach the right people. It is important to carefully screen the print publication to determine if it meets your needs. You can avoid costly mistakes by staying within your advertising budget and discussing advertisement costs and placement with your sales representatives.

ADVERTISING VEHICLES

Media Advertising

National network advertising is very powerful and, for the most part, is utilized by large businesses. The large network stations offer the most leverage to the advertiser because of the vast numbers of viewers and listeners.

Local Radio Advertising

Individuals may use local radio stations to attract clients. The service provider who draws a client base within a twenty mile radius would benefit from advertising on a local radio station. The business that sells a product or service on a regional or national level would be better serviced by a station with larger frequency.

Newspaper Advertisements

Most newspaper advertisements are targeted for local readers. Reading the local paper will help you understand the community. Knowing the needs of that community will help you meet the needs of the people.

Magazines and Trade Publications

Most magazines and trade publications have national

subscribers. When you write an advertisement for a national magazine, keep in mind that the community served is opened to all geographic locations.

Trade Shows

Trade shows and conventions are another way to get advertising leverage, as the traffic flow during these events ranges anywhere from several hundred to several thousand people. The strongest way to advertise a service or product is to have a booth at the show. Booths vary greatly in cost depending upon the size of the event, but the booth exhibit can more than pay for itself.

DIRECT MAIL

Direct mail is a form of leverage because one piece of information is sent out to masses of people. Successful direct mail campaigns depend upon the specifics of the data base: *the demographics of your target market*. Mailing list houses sell lists according to the following:

- *Residential*: Yellow pages, surveys, magazine and trade journal subscribers, for example. You can buy mailing lists according to your own specific demographic requirements such as location, make-up of family, age, income, and occupation.
- *Industrial*: Lists of corporations and businesses according to sales volume, numbers of employees, types of industry, location, and department heads.
- Some publications sell their own lists directly, which may or may not be preselected by demographics.

Most mailing houses have a set fee with a usual minimum of 5,000 names. If you want only 2,000 names, you can buy a duplicate of that list to use for another mailing, unless otherwise indicated by the mailing house.

The key to a successful and cost effective direct mail campaign is to target your market, develop a profile of clients and customers most likely to buy your service or product, and choose lists based on your profile.

Creating Your Own Mailing Lists

The following suggestions are proven ways to use your available resources to create your own mailing lists:

- Use the yellow pages by making a list of the service providers or institutions. You'll have to look up the zip codes, but it's a small price to pay for the most current listings offered by the yellow pages.
- Use resource books such as the manufacturers' guide of your particular state. You can develop your data base from these listings. Make sure that the resource book is current, as businesses constantly grow and change.
- Always collect names and addresses of people who know your work. These names create the best data base because those people have had direct contact with you.

Writing Direct Mail Pieces

The best way to solicit your services in writing is to research the market. I receive many letters from publications looking for subscribers. Although they are written by professional writers and advertising specialists, many of the concepts can be adapted in your letters. The library may provide you with resources. It might also pay to hire a public relations consultant to help you target your market and compose a direct mail piece.

The essential ingredients of the direct mail letter tell the reader who you are, what you offer, and why they need your service. Most direct mail pieces offer special rates or discounts. Another way to entice prospective clients is to offer your consulting services at a flat rate for a certain amount of time, such as a six month rate for "x" number of dollars. This gives the client the opportunity to develop a relationship with you.

Writing Your Advertisement

You need some basic information before you write an advertisement. The headline must tell the greatest benefit of your product or service. Look at advertisements of your colleagues or simply look at the advertising section of the local paper. The copy makes a clear and simple offer. It does not have to tell everything. It needs only to draw the attention and interest of the reader. An advertisement is only successful if it continues to bring in response. Remember, advertisements don't last unless they are working.

Size, Shape, and Position

The size, shape, and placement of the advertisement first attracts the reader. Here are facts to consider in placing your advertisement:

1. Advertisement Classification – The categories that match your service.
2. Advertisement Type – Size, shape, and length of the advertisement.
3. Advertisement Placement – Where the advertisement is placed in the newspaper or magazine.

You may also consider low-cost, or no-cost, advertising by publishing articles that promote your service, getting letters of reference from satisfied clients, or handing out flyers or business cards announcing your service.

It's important to give your advertisement some time to make an impact. Two to three months is the minimum amount of time to run the ad in a magazine. Results are faster in local newspapers. Your tracking system will eventually help you determine whether your money has been well spent.

To review, the key to advertising is to know yourself and your market. It all goes back to creating and believing

your vision. Then apply the QPN Model to understand
your qualities, purpose, and client needs.

**The tools and the vehicles of advertising are only
as powerful as your ability and willingness to use
them effectively.**

18

Promoting Yourself

*I*t's easy to explain a tangible product, such as computer software or a nutritional supplement, but harder to see your own intangible product as an artist, writer, consultant. The reason that it's difficult to "sell yourself" is that it often sounds and feels like you are boasting, and that if someone rejects your work they are rejecting you as a person.

SELLING THE INTANGIBLE YOU

This dilemma can be resolved by seeing your work as separate from yourself, "framing your work inside a billboard" and describing what you do in a detached state from your ego, as an outsider. Ego detachment doesn't mean that your work life and your inner life are not part of you. It means that you can differentiate your "being" from your "doing." And you can transmit this concept to your clients by explaining your work carefully and slowly, by using simple language. This shows your clients that you care about them, and reduces your own anxiety as a promoter. Your main goal is to help them understand your service.

157

THE QPN MODEL – YOUR GREAT PROMOTIONAL TOOL

The QPN Model comes in handy when you are selling yourself to your client. It also creates winning relationships. The purpose (P) of my work is to motivate people to help them get better jobs, have better relationships, and promote themselves and their products. They attend (N) my lectures and workshops for those reasons (P=N).

However, different audiences are attracted to different qualities. Some require a dynamic presentation, others need a more tutorial setting. In some groups, I am primarily a teacher. In others, I am more of a facilitator. Those are my qualities (Q) and I use the ones that meet the needs of my group.

In my role as a consultant, my general purpose (P) is to develop strategies to help my clients sell their products. They seek my services (N) for the same reason (P=N), and I emphasize the qualities that they need, such as efficiency and integrity (Q).

In promoting yourself to your clients, it is important to explain your service and the features you have to offer. Many times I was so enthusiastic in explaining my work that I forgot to ask about the clients's needs until later in the conversation. There is a delicate balance between explaining your services and the client explaining his needs, however, it's one that can be monitored by applying the QPN Model when promoting yourself to your clients.

CREATING WORD OF MOUTH

Word of mouth is a powerful and effective way to spread word about your work. But words are not enough. You also need longevity with clients. Make every effort to stay in touch with your customers by telephone or letter. Continuity does pay off. The following promotional materials will help you to create word of mouth:

BROCHURES

Brochures come in all shapes, sizes, and formats.

The brochure is your major marketing piece and should reflect your style and purpose. The content must clearly state your qualities (expressed as credibility), your purpose (expressed as the objective) and how you will meet the needs of the marketplace (expressed as a benefit statement to the reader). Your logo, quality of paper stock, choice of type, and spacing will all add to the quality of your brochure.

NEWSLETTERS
Newsletters are useful tools in which to stay in touch with your clients and customers. The more often they see your name, the more likely they are to refer you to others. The best audience for your newsletters are those people who already know your work. But you can expand your mailing list from your lectures, potential clients you meet at conventions and trade shows, and business cards exchanged at networking meetings.

Sample newsletters can also be sent to the targeted list of subscribers you buy from a mailing house or magazine. They are subtle forms of advertising because you are selling your skills and knowledge while offering subscribers valuable information.

Although it is important to charge a yearly fee for the newsletter, it becomes a tool to increase your business rather than a money maker on its own. You can encourage more subscribers by keeping the initial cost down and offering them an opportunity to send in interesting information, personal testimonies, and commentaries.

PRESS RELEASES
Press releases are informational pieces that tell the reader "who, what, where, when, why, and how" about an event or person. They can be less than a page or can be written in two or more pages if describing achievements or accomplishments. The purpose of a press release is to highlight the service, product, or person and state the "hook" that will grab the attention of the reader. Editors

often use press releases in the publication or as a lead for a story written about the subject.

PRESS KITS

Press kits are used by speakers, authors, consultants, and many other professionals to describe and give credibility to their work. Press kits vary in size and scope, but contain any or all of the following:

1. biography
2. brochures
3. published articles you have written
4. articles written about your work by someone else
5. testimonial letters
6. list of media appearances
7. promotional literature, such as flyers, catalogue descriptions, and book promotions

Public relations firms and promotional consultants favor press kits and can give you advice on how to put one together.

The portfolio differs from the press kit in that it is used to show tangible evidence of work such as the artist's drawings or the architect's designs. The portfolio can be purchased in an art supply store or in a leather goods shop.

LONG LASTING PROMOTERS

Here are no-cost strategies you can utilize:

1. Give free talks to clubs and organizations.
2. Sponsor a workshop in your home.
3. Have friends type your flyers on their computers.
4. Appear on radio and television talk shows.
5. Exchange leads and ideas with friends.
6. Barter your services.
7. Gather testimonial letters.
8. Have a reporter write about your work.
9. Write an article for the media.
10. Develop a mailing list.

It is important to keep track of responses to your promotional materials and techniques. You can ask people attending your lectures to fill out information cards with their names, address and phone number, and you can keep a record of which procedures work best for you. I also ask people to put the date and place of the lecture on the card and which of my topics was of interest to them.

SPEAKERS BUREAUS

Speakers bureaus work on behalf of the client who is requesting the speaker and paying the fee. If your material matches their client's needs, the speakers bureau will make all of the arrangements and take a percentage of the fee you agree on, which is usually twenty-five percent. It is beneficial to be on speaker lists, because it enhances your professional reputation and you can often receive expert advice from the consultant at the speakers bureau.

PUBLIC RELATIONS FIRMS

The public relations consultant works to promote you. He or she offers many services, including writing your promotional material, setting up media interviews, and generally publicizing your project. Fees are generally high, so make sure you find out exactly what you will get ahead of time. There are no guarantees in this business, but public relations will bring attention to your work and the exposure and well-developed materials can only enhance your image.

MARKETEERS

For the most part, public relations firms do not enroll people in your workshops or book your speaking engagements. And although speakers bureaus book speaking engagements, they do so on behalf of the client when there is a match of interests.

Finding a personal promoter is best. He or she must know your work and your materials in order to promote you. Some promoters work independently and are listed in the yellow pages and resource directories. Or you can ask a colleague for names.

WRITING AND PUBLISHING BOOKS

Get advice from an agent or an editor at a publishing company before you begin. Speak to many people to get ideas and strategies. Once you have determined your market, submit a proposal for your book. This includes an overview, a table of contents (annotated), and at least one chapter. Also include publicity material on yourself.

The difference between the agent and the publisher is the difference between the real estate broker and the home buyer. The agent works to sell your book. He finds the publisher and acts as a liaison. In most cases (although sometimes small), you will receive an advance against royalties on your book. The agent will take a percentage of your profits from the book as a commission.

You can also send your work directly to publishers, but you must write a query letter first in order to save time on your behalf, and on behalf of the publisher. If you do receive a contract without an agent, have a lawyer or book agent consultant review the terms.

Self-publishing is also possible. When you self-publish, you pay all costs, but you also receive all of the profits. You can also go to a "vanity press" and pay them to publish and promote your book.

Most of the big publishing houses have major distribution, but, for the most part, they will only promote your book at the outset. It is up to you to promote your own material. If your book doesn't sell, it will either sit on the shelf or be returned to the publisher. Don't discount the small publishers, especially if they have distribution networks. They have fewer authors to deal with, and will usually spend time to promote the book and check on distribution. Remember, regardless of the size of your publisher, the key to the success of your book is in the marketing and distribution process.

Audio and video tapes are a market all by themselves.

There are publishing houses that produce them exclusively. In most cases, the audio tape comes after a book, and is sold separately.

Audio tapes are more cost effective and accessible to the general audience than video tapes. The audio cassette can be played in the car or at home. Video tapes are especially effective for the corporate market. Corporations are moving away from live workshops and toward using video tapes for training. With the exception of exercise videos and demonstration videotapes, I feel that audio tapes reach a wider consumer market than video tapes, and that video tapes should be considered *after* successful audio tape distribution has been attained.

UNIQUENESS COUNTS

The phrase "edge over the competition" can be rephrased to "there is no competition, we are all unique."

> **Spending the time to nurture, develop, and promote your uniqueness is what makes you successful. The idea is not to reinvent the wheel, but instead to find a new niche for your service or product.**

In summary, the ingredients to successful self-marketing are caring for your work, using your resources to gain credibility and exposure, and keeping your belief and vision alive.

19

Consciousness In The Workplace

I equate consciousness in the workplace with ethics and integrity, which are often tested in the work environment. Our values, our attitudes, and our behaviors are mixed with those of others, and, many times, values are challenged. When the challenges become unmanageable, the question of change appears. Making a career change triggers survival issues, such as losing income, job, family, and a certain standard of living and lifestyle.

WHAT IS CONSCIOUSNESS?

It is the purpose of this chapter to explore alternatives that will help you recognize and respect your own values and find ways to harmonize them with the values of the company or organization.

The following are examples of when to begin speaking up at work:

- Working overtime too many days in a row takes you away from your family.

165

- Constant demands from your boss puts you days behind in your work.
- Unfair practices within the company violate your ethics.

The following are examples of when to *stop* speaking up:

- When you've said your piece to the right people.
- When you've put your statements in writing.
- When you realize that your values clash with those of the company and there is no way to reconcile the differences.

WHEN TO DO NOTHING

There are situations in which the only course of action you have is to let go. For example, let's say that the company is allocating funds for materials you feel are unnecessary and wasteful. The management is aware of your feelings and the feelings of others in your department. Since management is aware of the problem, there is nothing you can do by yourself. However, you can make an impact if the management asks for your support.

The following are examples of when to do nothing:

- When you know the attitudes and behavior of management won't change, because others have tried.
- When you know the attitudes and behavior of management won't change, because you have tried.
- When you have taken all the necessary steps to make a change, e.g. discussions, forums, letters, staff support teams, and the situation does not change.

WHEN TO ASK FOR HELP

Even the most proficient executives encounter "impossible" clients and situations. When you are working with a very difficult person who changes their mind seemingly all the time, has unpredictable behavior, and doesn't listen to reason, your inner-voices will tell you there is trouble ahead. Calling your colleagues and mentors can help. But if you try their suggestions without success, it may be time to confront the client and discuss the issues directly. If, after your discussion, you still feel frustrated and incomplete, it may be time to let the client go. You can refer them to someone else, unless you can find a way to maintain your equilibrium while working with the client. Remember, your values and sanity come first.

The following are examples of when to ask for help:

- When you often find yourself angry and frustrated with your client.
- When your heart isn't in your work.
- When you've reached a stalemate with your client.

WHEN TO MAKE A CHANGE

Here is a scenario where making a change makes good sense.

Tim's boss reprimands him in front of the staff. Tim meets with his boss and tells him that he feels devalued and humiliated in this situation. When the situation doesn't change, it's time for Tim to make a change. By accepting verbal abuse, Tim is not being true to himself. When Tim believes in himself, he believes that he will find a work situation where he is respected and valued. If Tim stays in an abusive situation, it debilitates his confidence and energy, thus affecting his ability to use his talents and skills.

The following are examples of when to make a change:

- The work environment is damaging your spirit.
- You are being verbally abused or harassed.

- You have discussed your options with family, colleague, consultant, or therapist.

THE INTERNAL SHIFT

Before you can take any of the steps outlined above, it is necessary to make the following internal shifts in your belief system:

- You have to know that you are worthy of the best possible job.
- You have to know that the best possible job is waiting for you.
- You have to believe that your skills are necessary to make a positive impact in your field.
- You have to know that through your self-expression, you are making a positive contribution to society.

Many of us are under the common misconception that a job should not be released until another one is in place. Remember the universal law that nature abhors a vacuum and that the old must be released in order to make room for the new. This doesn't mean that you have to quit your job tomorrow, but you can begin to release the job mentally and explore your options physically.

Although making this commitment is a challenge, it is at the core of every change. It shows your willingness to accept and trust that your highest good will be met. This concept of a higher power greater than ourselves is part of all religions. But religious preference is not the focus here. Once you have developed trust and faith, it will be easier to make the transition because you will automatically know and believe that the next "right" step will be offered to you.

The following stories are from my own personal experience and those of my friends and colleagues. They are business stories of integrity, ethics, faith, and trust against the odds.

Letting The Deal Go

Tom is a friend and entrepreneur who has created self-esteem tapes. He was approached by a major Japanese corporation to back his project. They offered him $3,000,000 and forty-nine percent ownership in the company, which meant that Tom would lose control of the future direction of the company. Although he was living off borrowed money from credit cards and had to temporarily stop tape production, he followed his ethic and refused the offer. Tom knew that another source would appear, and, within several weeks, other backers started to offer their financial support. He also took action on his own to successfully market the tapes.

The Ethical Responsibility Story

John, a vice president of Corporation Z, was a recovered alcoholic. Because of his drinking problem, there had been occasions in the past where he did not handle clients in a professional manner. He joined Alcoholics Anonymous and, within several months, had stopped drinking. His professional behavior returned to a normal pattern within six months.

During this difficult period, John confided his problem to one of the corporate officers. There was a new opportunity for John to be assigned a special project. His confidant made a decision to bring up John's problem at the board meeting. Several weeks before the meeting, the officer told John he could not support his assignment to the new project based on John's problems with alcohol. He told John it was his "moral and ethical" responsibility to discuss his views with the board.

John gave the situation careful consideration and decided to risk the disclosure of his alcohol problem at the meeting, feeling that it showed his integrity and commitment to his recovery. John was willing to risk his standing with his peers.

Although he lost the special assignment that year, John was rewarded with it the following year. He was willing to stand up for his integrity, and, thus, he gained the trust of his colleagues.

Leaning On Moral Principles

Elaine directed public relations for a large computer company. She worked closely with the president, frequently working overtime without compensation. This contradicted her ethics, and she told the president how she felt. He told her that she either had to come in on Saturday or not to show up on Monday. Elaine left the company, but, three weeks later, the president called and asked her to come back. But, by then, it was too late. She had already been hired by another firm. This is an example of "putting your money where your values are."

JEOPARDIZING INTEGRITY

The following patterns can develop when your job isn't working for you. Look at these as warning signals that you should take a long hard look at the personal issues behind these behaviors.

1. Making excessive personal phone calls on the job.
2. Charging calls to the company without clearance.
3. Taking long business lunches.
4. Complaining constantly about the company.
5. Using your position to intimidate other employees.

SUPPORTING INTEGRITY

Find role models in the workplace whom you admire. Stick with the leaders, or those who set a good example for the company. Your mentor should be someone who takes a vested interest in your career and in whom you can show your vulnerability. Finding the right mentor opens up the "trust barrier" that is created when there is no one in which to confide.

Another way to support your integrity is to encourage other people. Use your strengths, such as character, integrity, responsibility and fairness to set the example for others.   You will gain tremendous support from people who emulate your positive qualities.

You can also bring your consciousness and values to those meetings where people are allowed and encouraged to state their views and share their ideas. Work within a structure to solve problems. This team approach is a very empowering vehicle for the individual member and for the team as a whole.

KEEPING YOUR INTEGRITY ALONG WITH YOUR JOB

The manner in which you deliver your message at work is a critical factor in gaining respect for your ideas and values. It's important to state how your ideas and plans will make a contribution to the company and how the plan will benefit the people involved.

By keeping that objectivity when you express your view, you become an integral part of the group, not a power seeker.   And there are those people with "seemingly strong egos" who became threatened by other people's power and use their own power to intimidate others.   They will gain respect for you by seeing your strong commitment to your views, and by feeling your respect for them. This respect comes from your acceptance of who they are, not necessarily in your agreement or disagreement with their views.

PROGRAMMING YOUR PRINCIPLES

The following are ways to "program" your beliefs and principles into your work:

1. Maintain a constant vision of the way you want it to be.
2. Use your power of intuition.   Trust the voice within.
3. Find colleagues who are positive catalysts who will help move you to the next place.
4. Challenge all limited beliefs.

5. Embrace your competition, knowing that there is none. In your uniqueness, you stand alone.
6. Constantly seek ways to make your business and/or your job better.

It is possible to maintain your value system, integrity, and ethics in the workplace. I'm not saying it is easy, but I believe that, if you stay true to your principles, the right doors will be opened for you to find a better job and a better opportunity. It's a matter of vision and a lot of faith.

20

Integrating
The Pieces

*M*aking your dream a reality comes from visualizing your wants. It also comes from a core belief that what you need and desire is already internalized within you. Therefore, through purpose and persistence, you can manifest your internal vision into the external world. I am convinced that success can be created without strife, and that winning relationships are a part of the process. This is a new way to express the concepts and values currently recognized throughout the business world.

Vision is both essence and form. Essence is intangible; form provides us with specific content. We must see the vision first. Then we can go back and create it. Sometimes, however, it is blocked. This comes from old tapes playing in our mind. We must release these old ideas and replace them with fresh, new tapes.

Remember to explore the needs of the market by defining the market you are trying to reach. The QPN Model identifies the three facets of the self-marketing process.

The Q in the QPN Model means qualities, which are our specific personal qualities that match the needs of the client. The P in the QPN Model means purpose, which is the sum total of our goals, dreams and visions. Our purpose is stated as a positive thought in the present tense. The N in the QPN Model stands for needs. Here we determine how the service will benefit the client by going back to the qualities listed. Then we must conduct both subjective and objective research before we select a specific client or target. The QPN Model is a vital component of the marketing process.

Through the process of vision, we choose an ultimate outcome. For example, we already know a sale will take place, if we have a successful relationship with a client. It all happens ahead of time. Choosing the outcome means no more than making a conscious choice to act, involving stating the choice, seeing it and sensing it. The more we can vividly see the pictures, the greater the chance we have of making them a reality. We then, "become the image we believe" by "being it" before "we are it". This involves stretching ourselves to act out the next step, which often gives us an uneasy feeling. Our mentors and support systems can help us take small steps, maintaining the constant vision, and "surrender" knowing that we have taken the necessary action. We can then give up pushing and flow with the energy that moves us toward our goals.

Integral to being a success in business is the ability to receive non-verbal information by using our intuition. When we develop rapport with our clients, we can meet our needs and those of the client by using trust, receptivity, and listening skills. Also important is the ability to understand and interpret the words that clients and colleageus use that can set up limiting beliefs and negative patterns. Words are very powerful. When we say, "This is impossible," we automatically create an impossible situation. Words are an expression of our thought forms which we must choose carefully. And "word power" is an essential part of communication.

Life is an accumulation of how one spends one's hours. Try going beyond your appointment book and daily agenda to focus on priorities, purposes and goals as they relate to time management. The most successful people master their time and make it work for them. They also relax their minds and clear out old thoughts, making way for new ideas. By matching activities to priorities, we create our own measure of how time is used.

The powerful concept of leverage can be applied to our promotional materials, marketing strategies and advertising, so that we can reach many people through a single effort. But the key to any long term success and well-being depends on developing and maintaining balance between the many roles we play. Work, play, sleep, relationships, hobbies, or just sitting around are all vital to a balanced life. We can learn how to weigh the evidence by learning to take an "aerial view" of our lives. By standing "over the top" of our day, we gain perspective and are better able to see what is missing or what looms too large, and how to arrange our lives for better balance and a greater chance of long-term happiness.

The greatest successes come from our ability to make mistakes and transform them into valuable lessons. A mistake usually encompasses wrong timing, wrong strategy, or the wrong market. A clue is always evident just before the mistake occurs that we somehow miss. When the mistake is made, there is an immediate lesson to be learned, and the lesson becomes the fertile soil for new growth.

I have met many inspired people over the years who have incredible genius but very little foresight as to how to spread the word of their ideas. And I have met other successful people who are not inspired, and gain their success by manipulating situations and others. It is my goal to stimulate readers to create a working system that combines business success with internal satisfaction and peace.

In the material presented here, utilize the suggestions that work for you, but use your own thoughts to mold the ideas to your specific needs. There is no set pattern for success. Lessons can be learned from all successful people. Try to integrate the best of all your experiences and you are bound to make your dreams come true.

APPENDIX

BIBLIOGRAPHY

American Health Magazine, Joel Gurin, Editor-In-Chief, 28 West 23rd Street, New York, New York 10010

Anderson, Nancy. *Work with Passion: How to do What You Love for a Living.* New York: Carroll and Graf Publishers, 1984.

Ardell, Donald. *High Level Wellness.* New York: Bantam Books, 1978.

Bandler, Richard and Grinder, John. *Frogs into Princes – Neuro Linguistic Programming.* Moab: Real People Press, 1979.

Bandler, Richard. *Using Your Brain – For a CHANGE.* Moab: Real People Press, 1985.

Beierle, Herbert L. *Success and Health Conscious Thoughts and Actions for Business People.* Campo: University of Healing Press, 1982.

Bender, James F. *How To Sell Well – The Art and Science of Professional Salesmanship.* New York: McGraw-Hill Book Company, Inc., 1961.

Benson, Herbert. *Relaxation Response.* New York: Avon Books, 1975.

Bliss, Edwin C. *Doing It Now.* New York: Bantam Books, Inc., 1984.

Bloomfield, Harold H., M.D. and Felder, Leonard Ph.D. *The Achilles Syndrome – Transforming Your Weakness into Strengths.* New York: Random House, 1985.

Bloomfield, Harold H., M.D. *The Holistic Way to Health and Happiness.* New York: Simon and Schuster, 1978.

Bly, Bob. *Ads that Sell.* Brentwood: Caddylak Systems, 1988.

Body, Mind Spirit Magazine, Paul Zuromski, Editor-In-Chief and Publisher, P.O.Box 701, Providence, Rhode Island 02901

Branden, Nathaniel, Ph.D. *To See What I See and Know What I Know:A Guide to Self Discovery.* New York: Bantam Books, Inc., 1986.

Brannen, William H. *Advertising and Sales Promotion:Cost Effective Techniques for Your Small Business.* Englewood Cliffs: Prentice Hall, 1983.

Bristol, Claude M. *The Magic of Believing – The Science of*

Setting Your Goal and Then Reaching It. New York: Prentice Hall Press, 1986.

Burka, Jane. *Procrastination: Why You Do It, What To Do About It.* Reading: Addison-Wesley Publishing Co., 1990.

Buscaglia, Leo, Ph.D. *Living, Loving and Learning.* New York: Ballantine Books, 1982.

Carnegie, Dale and Carnegie, Dorothy. *How To Win Friends and Influence People, Rev. Ed.* New York: Simon and Schuster, Inc., 1981.

Chopra, Deepak, M.D. *Quantum Healing.* New York: Bantam Books, 1989.

Colbin, Annemarie. *Book of Whole Meals.* New York: Ballantine Books, 1979, 1983.

Colbin, Annemarie. *Food and Healing.* New York: Ballantine Books, 1986.

Cole-Whittaker, Terry. *The Inner Path From Where You Are to Where You Want To Be – A Spiritual Odyssey.* New York: Ballantine Books, 1986.

Cole-Whittaker, Terry. *How to Have More In a Have-Not World.* New York: Fawcett Crest, 1983.

Crum, Thomas F. *The Magic of Conflict: Turning a Life of Work Into a Work of Art.* New York: Simon and Schuster, Inc., 1987.

Cypert, Samuel A. *Believe and Achieve – W.Clement Stone's New Success Formula.* New York: Dodd, Mead & Company, 1987.

Dayhoff, Signe. *Create Your Own Career Opportunities.* Acton: Brick House Publishing Co., 1987.

Dossey, Larry. *Space, Time, and Medicine.* Boston: Shambhala Publishing, Inc., 1982.

Drury, N., ed. *Inner Health: The Health Benefits of Relaxation, Meditation and Visualization.* San Leandro: Prison Press, 1985.

Dyer, Wayne W.,Ph.D. *The Sky's The Limit.* New York: Simon and Schuster, 1980.

Dyer, Wayne W., Ph.D. *You'll See It When You Believe It.* New York: William Morrow & Co., 1989.

Earth Star, Whole Life New England, Lane Masterson, Editor, P.O.Box 110, Temple, New Hampshire 03084

Edwards, Betty. *Drawing on the Right Side of the Brain.* Los Angeles: Jeremy P. Tarcher, Inc., 1989.

Ferguson, Marilyn. *The Aquarian Conspiracy – Personal and Social Transformation in the 1980's*. Los Angeles: Jeremy P. Tarcher, Inc., 1980.

Forbes, Rosalind, Ed.D. *Corporate Stress*. Garden City: Doubleday & Company, Inc., 1979.

Fox, Emmet. *Make Your Life Worthwhile*. San Francisco: Harper & Row, Publishers, 1946.

Foyder, Joan Ellen. *Family Caregiver's Guide: The Home Health Care System that Really Works*. Cincinnati: Futuro, 1987.

Garfield, Charles. *Peak Performers: The New Heroes of America*. New York: Avon Books, 1987.

Gawain, Shakti. *Creative Visualization*. New York: Bantam Books, 1982.

Gawain, Shakti. *Living In The Light – A Guide to Personal and Planetary Transformation*. Mill Valley: Whatever Publishing, 1986.

Gelb, Michael J. *Present Yourself: Captivate Your Audience with Great Presentation Skills*. Rolling Hills Estates: Jalmer Press, 1988.

Gershon, David, and Gail Straub. *Empowerment: The Art of Creating Life as You Want*. New York: Delacorte Press, 1989.

Gifford, Susan Jean, Editor. *Choices and Connections*. Boulder: Human Potential Resources, Inc., 1988.

Gillies, Jerry. *Moneylove: How to Get the Money You Deserve for Whatever You Want*. New York: M. Evans, and Co. Inc., 1988.

Goldberg, Phillip. *Intuitive Edge: Understanding Intuition and Applying it in Everyday Life*. Los Angeles: Jeremy P. Tarcher, Inc., 1985.

Gordon, Thomas Dr. *Leader Effectiveness Training L.E.T. – The No-Lose Way to Release the Productive Potential of People,* New York: Bantam Books, 1984.

Goss, Frederick D. *$uccess in New$letter Publishing, A Practical Guide*. The Newsletter Association, 1985.

Greenwald, Jerry Dr. *Be the Person You Were Meant to Be – Antidotes to Toxic Living*. New York: Dell Publishing, 1973.

Hay, Louise. *Heal Your Body*. Santa Monica: Hay House, 1982, 1984.

Hill, Napoleon and Stone, W. Clement. *Success Through a*

Positive Mental Attitude. New York: Pocket Books, 1987.

Hobbs, Charles R. *Time Power: The Revolutionary Time Management System that Can Change Your Professional and Personal Life.* New York: Harper and Row Publishing, Inc., 1988.

Hopkins, Tom. *The Official Guide to Success – Volume One.* Scottsdale: Tom Hopkins International, Inc., 1982.

Horowitz, Sheldon. *Keep Your Money: How to Save Thousands In Advertising.* Northampton: Writing and More, 1985.

Howard, Vernon. *The Mystic Path to Cosmic Power.* West Nyack: Parker Publishing Company,Inc., 1967.

Howe, E. W. *Success Easier than Failure.* Irvine: Reprint Series Corp., 1988.

Ingenito, Marcia Gervase. *National New Age Yellow Pages.* Fullerton, California. 1987, 1988, 1991.

Jackson, Gerald and Townley, Roderick. *The Inner Executive: Access Your Intuition For Business Success.* New York: Pocket Books, Inc., 1989.

Jaffe, Dennis T., Ph.D. and Scott, Cynthia D., Ph.D. *From Burnout to Balance – A Workbook for Peak Performance and Self-Renewal.* New York: McGraw-Hill Book Company, 1984.

Jampolsky, Gerald G. M.D. *Teach Only Love – The Seven Principles of Attitudinal Healing.* New York: Bantam Books, 1983.

Kassorla, Irene C. Dr. *Go For It! – How to Win at Love, Work and Play.* New York: Dell Publishing, 1984.

Kohn, Alfie. *No Contest – The Case Against Competition.* Boston: Houghton Mifflin Co., 1986.

Laborde, Genie Z. *Influencing With Integrity: Management Skills for Communication and Negotiation.* Palo Alto: Syntony Publishing, Inc., 1988.

Lakelin, Alan. *How To Get Control of Your Time and Your Life.* Boston: Bulfinch Press, 1989.

LeBoeuf, Michael. *How to Win Customers and Keep them for Life.* New York: Berkley Publishing Group, 1989.

LeBoeuf, Michael. *Working Smart: How to Accomplish More in Half the Time.* New York: Warner Books, Inc., 1980.

LeShan, Lawrence. *How to Meditate*. New York: Bantam Books, 1974.

Magical Blend Magazine, Michael Peter Langevin, Editor, P.O.Box 11303, San Francisco, California 94101

Maltz, Maxwell M.D. *Psycho-cybernetics – A New Way to Get More Living Out of Life*. North Hollywood: Wilshire Book Company, 1960.

Mandino, Og. *The Greatest Salesman in the World*. New York: Bantam Books, 1968.

Marks, Linda. *Living With Vision: Reclaiming the Power of the Heart*. Indianapolis: Knowledge Systems, Inc., 1988.

Milwid, Beth, Ph.D. *What You Get When You Go For It*. New York: Dodd, Mead and Company, 1987.

Naisbitt, John and Aburdene, Patricia. *Megatrends 2000 – Ten New Directions for the 1990's*. New York: William Morrow and Company, Inc., 1990.

Naisbitt, John. *Megatrends – Ten New Directions Transforming Our Lives*. New York: Warner Books, 1984.

Nelson Bolles, Richard. *What Color Is Your Parachute? – A Practical Manual for Job-Hunters & Career Changers*. Berkeley: Ten Speed Press, 1984.

New Age Journal, Peggy Taylor, Editor, 342 Western Avenue, Brighton, Massachusetts 02135

New Age Marketing Opportunities Newsletter, First Editions, P.O. Box 2568, Sedona, Arizona 86336

Nightingale, Earl. *Earl Nightingale's Greatest Discovery: The Strangest Secret...Revisited*. New York: Dodd, Mead, and Co., 1987.

Noe, John R. *Peak Performance Principles for High Achievers*. New York: Berkley Publishing Group, 1989.

Ornish, Dean M.D. *Stress, Diet and Your Heart*. New York: Holt, Rinehart and Winston, 1982.

Patent, Arnold M. *You Can Have It All – The Art of Winning the Money Game and Living a Life of Joy*. Great Neck: Money Mastery Publishing, 1984.

Paul, Shale. *Warrior Within: A Guide to Inner Power*. Evergreen: Delta Group Press, 1984.

Paulsen, Pat A., Brown, Sharon C., and Wolf, Jo Ann. *Living on Purpose*. New York: Simon and Schuster, Inc., 1988.

Peale, Norman Vincent. *Positive Imaging: The Powerful*

Way to Change Your Life. Old Tappan: Revell, Flemming, and Co., 1981.

Pelletier, Kenneth R. *Holistic Medicine – From Stress to Optimum Health.* New York: Dell Publishing, 1979.

Peters, Thomas J. and Waterman, Robert H. Jr. *In Search of Excellence – Lessons from America's Best-Run Companies.* New York: Harper & Row, Publishers, 1982.

Poppe, Fred. *Fifty Rules to Keep a Client Happy.* New York: Harper and Row, Publishers, 1987.

Potter, Beverly. *Way of the Ronin: A Guide to Career Strategy.* New York: Amacom, 1984.

Potter, Beverly. *Way of the Ronin: Riding the Waves of Change at Work.* Berkeley: Ronin Publishing, Inc., 1989.

Price, John Randolph. *The Superbeings.* New York: Ballantine Books, 1981.

Robbins, Anthony. *Unlimited Power.* New York: Ballantine Books, 1986.

Roman, Sanaya and Packer, Duane. *Creating Money – Keys to Abundance.* Tiburon: H.J.Kramer Inc., 1988.

Rosanoff, Nancy. *Intuition Workout: A Practical Guide to Discovering and Developing Your Inner Knowing.* Arlington: Aslan Press, 1988.

Ross, Ruth, Ph.D. *Prospering Woman – A Complete Guide to Achieving the Full, Abundant Life.* San Rafael: New World Library, 1982.

Rowan, Roy. *The Intuitive Manger.* Boston: Little, Brown and Company, 1986.

Ryan, Tim and Case, Patricia J. *The Whole Again Resource Guide.* Santa Barbara: SourceNet, 1987.

Sachs, Laura. *Do-It Yourself Marketing for the Professional Practice.* Englewood Cliffs: Prentice Hall, Inc., 1986.

Scheale, Adele M. *Skills for Success.* New York: Ballantine Books, Inc., 1987.

Schuller, Robert H. *Getting Through: The Going Through Stage.* New York: Ballantine Books, Inc., 1988.

Schuller, Robert H. *Success is Never Ending – Failure is Never Final.* Boston: G. K. Hall and Co., 1989.

Schwartz, David J. *The Magic of Getting What You Want.* New York: William Morrow and Company, Inc., 1983.

Scott, Dewitt H. *Getting Favorable Publicity: The Marketing Tool That Costs You Nothing.* Los Alamitos: Duncliffs International, 1985.

Sharing Ideas, Walters Speaking Services, P.O. Box 1120, Glendora, California 91740

Sher, Barbara. *Wishcraft:How to Get What You Really Want.* New York: Ballantine Books, 1979.

Sinetar, Marsha. *Do What You Love The Money Will Follow – Discovering Your Right Livelihood.* New York: Paulist Press, 1987.

Smith, Leroy Jr. *The Science of Personal Success: How to Turn Your Life Into a World of Endless Success.* Columbia: Prestige Enterprise, 1985.

Smith-Jones, Susan. *Choose To Be Healthy – Discover How to Embrace Life and Live Fully.* Berkeley: Celestial Arts, 1987.

Stone, W. Clement. *The Success System That Never Fails.* Englewood Cliffs: Prentice-Hall, Inc. 1962.

Success Magazine, Scott DeGarmo, Editor, 342 Madison Avenue, New York, New York 10173

Thomas, Christina. *Secrets: A Practical Guide to Undreamed of Possibilities.* Memphis: Chela Publishers, 1989.

Thomas, David A. *There Are No Dragons Out There: The Miracle of You and What You Can Become.* Salt Lake City: Olympus Publishing Co., 1986.

Tracy, Brian. *The Psychology of Selling.* Chicago: Nightingale Conant Corp., 1988.

Travis, John W. M.D. and Callander, Meryn G. *Wellness For Helping Professionals – Creating Compassionate Cultures.* Mill Valley: Wellness Associates Publications, 1990.

Travis, John W. M.D. and Ryan, Regina Sara. *The Wellness Workbook – Second Edition.* Berkeley: Ten Speed Press, 1981, 1988.

Vaughan, Frances E. *Awakening Intuition.* New York: Doubleday and Co. Inc., 1979.

Viladas, Luise. *Advertising that Pays for Itself.* Greenwich: Havemeyer Books, 1987.

Waitley, Denis E. and Tucker, Robert B. *Winning the Innovation Game.* Old Tappan: Fleming H. Revell Company, 1986.

Walters, Dottie and Walters, Lillet. *Speak and Grow Rich.* Englewood Cliffs: Prentice Hall, 1989.

Walther, George R. *Phone Power.* New York: Putnam Publishing Groups, 1986.

Walton, Mary. *Deming Management Method.* New York: Putman Publishing Group, 1986.

Warschaw, Tessa Albert, Ph.D. *Rich is Better – How Women Can Bridge the Gap Between Wanting and Having It All: Financially, Emotionally, Professionally.* Garden City: Doubleday & Co., 1985.

Warschaw, Tessa Albert, Ph.D. *Winning By Negotiation.* New York: Berkley Books, 1981.

Weinstein, Marion. *Positive Magic – Occult Self-Help.* Custer: Phoenix Publishing Inc., 1980.

Wilson, Larry and Hersch Wilson. *Changing the Game: The New Way to Sell.* New York: Simon and Schuster, Inc., 1987.

Witcher, William. *You Can Spend Less and Sell More: The Advertising Book.* Scotts Valley: Mark Publishing Inc., 1988.

Zacharies, James L. *Letting Go and Having It All.* Lakewood: Stepping Stones Press, 1986.

Ziglar, Zig. *See You At The Top.* Gretna: Pelican Publishing Co., Inc., 1984.

Ziglar, Zig. *Top Performance.* Old Tappan: Fleming H. Revell Company, 1986.

Zuromski, Paul. "How to Improve Your Advertising." *Body, Mind, and Spirit Magazine.* Providence, Rhode Island. 1987.

Zuromski, Paul, and Editors of Body Mind Spirit Magazine. *The New Age Catalogue.* Dolphin: Doubleday, New York, New York, 1988.

RESOURCE DIRECTORIES

Daniells, Lorna M., *BUSINESS INFORMATION SOURCES – Rev. Ed.,* University Of California Press, 1985.

This book is a guide to vast and varied sources of business information for the business professional, business student and librarians. It is the most comprehensive collection of resource material in one publication. Ms. Daniells is in the process of revising the 1985 edition.

The references listed below are taken from this book with permission of the publisher.

ABI/INFORM database
Database covering primarily English-language journals in the area of business/management.

**Business Organizations, Agencies
and Publications Directory.**
Gale Research Co., 4th ed., 1988, 2 volumes
This directory covers major trade and business organizations, government agencies, commodity and stock exchanges, labor unions, chambers of commerce, diplomatic representation, trade and convention centers, trade fairs, franchise companies, hotel/motel systems, publishers, data banks and computerized services, educational institutions, business libraries and information centers and research centers.

Consultants and Consulting Organizations Directory.
Gale Research Co., in Detroit, Mich., 2 volumes (triennial, with annual supplements)
This is a comprehensive worldwide directory of consulting firms, offering all types of business services, and giving for each: top officers, branch offices, type of service offered.

Directory of Corporate Affiliations.
The National Register Publishing Co., in Wilmette, IL. (annual with bimonthly supplements)
Section 1 is a cross-reference index for all subsidiaries, divisions, etc. of major American parent companies listed in Section 2 showing line of business, approximate sales, number of employees, ticker symbol, top officers, subsidiaries, divisions or affiliates. The International Directory of Corporate Affiliations is an annual companion volume in three sections.

Directory of Executive Recruiters
Kennedy Publications in Fitzwilliam, N.H. (annual)
This directory lists retainer recruiting firms and contingency recruiters. Indexes are by function, industry and

geographic location. Other publications include International Directory of Executive Recruiters and the Directory of Outplacement Firms.

Dun's Marketing Services – America's Corporate Families.
Parsippany, N.J. (annual)
The white pages contain a select list of U.S. "ultimate parent companies" with their U.S. divisions and subsidiaries. The data is similar to the Dun's Million Dollar Directory. A companion volume is America's Corporate Families and International Affiliates (annual) containing a two part list of Canadian and foreign subsidiaries and U.S. subsidiaries of foreign and Canadian parent companies.

Dun's Marketing Services – Million Dollar Directory
Parsippany, N.J. – 5 Volumes (annual) The three volume set contains a listing of U.S. businesses, each worth over $500,000. Each business listing includes officers and directors, line of business, SIC codes, approximate sales, number of employees, stock exchange abbreviations, principal bank, accounting firm and legal counsel among others. 3 unnumbered volumes contain the listings. Volumes 4-5 are "Series Cross-Reference Volumes," one by geographic location; the other by 4-digit SIC industry.

Encyclopedia of Associations
by Gale Research Co. in Detroit Michigan. 3 volumes in 5 parts (annual)
The key Volume 1, in 3 parts, contains a comprehensive list of all types of "national organizations of the US" arranged in broad categories. Each association lists activities, number of members, publications, dates of meetings, etc. They now publish a companion set: Encyclopedia of Associations: International Organizations, 2 volumes.

Foundation Directory
Foundation Center (biennial) in New York.
A directory of U.S. foundations with assets of $1 million

and over, arranged by state and including the following data for each: date of incorporation, donors, purpose and activities, financial statistics, officers, directors and trustees, grant application information. They also publish an annual and bimonthly Foundation Grants Index.

Gale Directory of Publications and Broadcast Media
Detroit, Gale Research Co. annual. 3 Volumes
This geographic list of newspapers, magazines and trade publications is over 100 years old and covers periodicals published in the U.S., Canada, U.S. possessions and territories. Information includes editor, year founded, frequency, subjects covered, circulation, subscription and advertising rates.

Oxbridge Directory of Newsletters
Oxbridge Communications Inc., in New York (biennial)
This is a specialized comprehensive list of U.S. and Canadian newsletters, arranged by subject, and with an alphabetical index. Each publication contains references to editor, frequency, price, description of editorial content, distribution of readership as well as length of issue.

Standard & Poor Register of Corporations, Directors and Executives. New York: Standard & Poor's Corp. 3 volumes
(with three cumulated supplements)
Volume 1. alphabetical listing companies.
Volume 2. contains brief data about each executive and director.
Volume 3. contains various indexes and lists, by geographic location, companies added for the first time and first time offices and an obituary section.

Standard Directory of Advertisers
The National Register Publishing Co. in Wilmette, Ill. (annual, with monthly cumulated supplements)
This Directory contains companies that advertise nationally, arranged by industry, with an alphabetical index. The listing includes officers, top sales personnel,

products, advertising agency, and media used. Their
"Tradename Index" and "Geographic Index" are in
separate volumes. A new companion volume is the
Standard Directory of Worldwide Marketing listing
both foreign advertisers and foreign advertising agencies.

Standard Directory of Advertising Agencies
National Register Publisher Co., Wilmette, Ill. (annual).
Contains specialization, officers, account executives, approximate annual billings, % by media, names of ac-
counts and ranking for the top 25 largest agencies.
They now publish a new companion volume: the
Standard Directory of Worldwide Marketing which
lists both foreign advertisers and foreign advertising
agencies.

Standard Periodical Directory
Oxbridge Communications, Inc. in New York (annual)
Contains the publication source for a particular periodical,
Includes top personnel, circulation, frequency,
printer, and advertising specifications.

Ulrich's International Periodicals Directory
by R.R. Bowker, New York. 3 volumes (biennial)
This directory lists, by subject, both foreign and domestic periodicals. Data includes frequency, subscription rate, circulation and whether it includes book re-
views, statistics, indexing or is indexed by a regular
service.

World Guide to Trade Associations
K.G.Saur, 1985, 3d.ed. in Munich & New York, 1259 pp.
This guide contains national and international trade associations and professional associations, chambers of
commerce, etc.

MEDIA SOURCES
Bacon's Radio and TV Directory
Bacon's Publishing Co. Chicago (annual) Listing of over
10,000 radio and TV stations, call letters, addresses,

phone, key personnel, programs, times broadcast, name of contacts, network affiliations, frequency or channel numbers, target audience data.

Bacon's Publicity Checker
Chicago, Bacon's Publishing Co. (annual) with quarterly supplements.
Listing of trade and consumer magazines, daily and weekly newspapers in the U.S. and Canada.

Broadcasting/Cable Yearbook
Broadcasting Publications in Washington, D.C.
Contains a wealth of directory information, including data on U.S. and Canadian television and radio (AM and FM) stations, advertising agencies, networks and programming, cable systems, etc.

Working Press of the Nation 1988
five volume set
I. newspaper directory, II. magazine directory, III. TV and radio directory, IV. feature writers and photographers directory and V. international publications directory
Features syndicates, and daily and weekly newspapers, radio and television stations, magazines, feature writers and photographers, and internal house organs.

Yearbook of Experts, Authorities & Spokespersons, 8th Edition, Mitchell P. Davis, Editor, Broadcast Interview Source, 2233 Wisconsin Avenue N.W., Washington, D.C. 20007
A list of experts in a variety of topics indexed by topics, location and organization. Used by America's leading editors, reporters, news directors and radio-TV producers. Other publications include Power Media Selects and Talk Show Selects.

ORGANIZATIONS
N.A.P.R.A., New Age Publishing and Retailing Alliance, Marilyn McGuire, Ex. Director, P.O. Box 9, Eastsound, Washington 98245
N.S.A, Nichiren Shosu Soka Gakkai of America, World Culture Center, 525 Wilshire Boulevard, Santa Mon-

ica,California 90401

N.S.A., National Speakers Association, 4747 N. 7th Street, Suite 310, Phoenix, Arizona 85014

National Wellness Association, University of Wisconsin – Stevens Point, Stevens Point, Wisconsin 54481

National Wellness Coalition, P.O. Box 3778, Washington, D.C. 20007

P.R.S.A., Public Relations Society of America, 845 Third Avenue, New York, New York 10022

QUARTUS FOUNDATION, P.O.Box 1768, Bourne, Texas 78006-6768

The Stress Management Counseling Center. Alan Elkin, Ph.D., Director. 110 East 36th Street, New York, New York 10016.

MAILING LISTS

MDS Media Distribution Services PRA Group, 307 West 36th St., New York, New York. 10018

NAM, New Age Mailing List, P.O.Box 970, Santa Cruz, New Mexico 87567

NEW AGE RESOURCES

Tarila, Sophia, Ph.D., *New Marketing Opportunities*, Volumes I and II, second edition, P.O. Box 2568, Sedona, Arizona 86336, First Editions, 1990-1991.

This comprehensive trade directory targets the metaphysical, new age, holistic, and consciousness marketplace. Vol. I contains almost 5,000 listings of metaphysical bookstores, crystal stores, visionary art galleries, music stores, speciality stores, and Canadian retailers and catalogs. Volume II contains extensive connections of book, periodical, audio and video publishers and producers; associations and networks; media connections; distributors and wholesalers; service; events and mailing lists.

MOTIVATIONAL TAPES AND SEMINARS

Career Track, 3085 Center Green Drive, Boulder, Colorado 80301-5408

Nightingale-Conant Corporation, 7300 North Lehigh Avenue, Chicago, Illinois 60648.

BRAIN-MIND RESEARCH

Acoustic Brain Research, Inc., P.O. Box 3214, Chapel Hill, North Carolina 27515

Effective Learning Systems, Inc., 5221 Edina Ind. Blvd., Edina, MN 55439

The Monroe Institute, Route 1, P.O. Box 175, Faber, Virginia 22938

MARKETING NEWSLETTERS AND REPORTS

The Marketing Communications Report, by Pete Silver, 4300 N.W. 23 Avenue, Suite 528, P.O.Box 1702-528, Gainesville, Florida 32602-1702

Marketing Genius At Work, Reports by Jay Abraham, P.O. Box 709, Waitsfield, Vermont 06673

The Kiplinger Washington Letter, The Kiplinger Washington Editors, 1729 H. Street N.W., Washington, D.C. 20006-3938

Sharing Ideas, Walters Speaking Services, P.O. Box 1120, Glendora, California 91740

The Bodywork Entrepreneur, by David Palmer, 584 Castro Street, # 373, San Francisco, California 94114

ABOUT THE AUTHORS –

Patricia J. Raskin, M. Ed., is a marketing consultant, motivational speaker and cable television host. She holds a Masters Degree in Counseling and has worked as a teacher and guidance counselor. As president of Raskin Resources, she has extensive experience in sales, marketing and public relations. She resides in Cheshire, Connecticut.

Ms. Raskin applies her skills in business where she is working as a consultant with ActionSystems, Inc., an international training and consulting firm. Alternatively, she takes her personalized marketing programs to holistic health conferences, schools and practitioners throughout the country and has made editorial contributions to *Earth Star Magazine, The Massage Therapy Journal* and *Body, Mind, Spirit Magazine.*

In her cable television program, "Making It Your Business", Ms. Raskin interviews entrepreneurs, business and health professionals to help viewers gain practical business information as well as experience successful role models. Her goal is to stimulate a creative working system which combines business success with internal satisfaction and peace.

Ms. Raskin helps her clients to understand and appreciate their own internal skills and then to apply them externally through self-marketing techniques that expand from time-management and communication skills to making the right media contacts and writing marketing materials.

For questions of further information about Ms. Raskin's seminars and consultations, please contact Roundtable Publishing, Inc., 29169 Heathercliff Road, Malibu, CA 90265.

NOTES

NOTES

NOTES

NOTES

NOTES

NOTES

NOTES

NOTES

NOTES

NOTES